MAYER SMIT

A Court of ashes and embers

Contents

I

Part One

The Spark of Flame

1

Whispers in the Dark

Ivy's breath caught in her throat as the door creaked open. The sound was barely audible, but it might as well have been thunder in the silence of the hallway. She stepped forward, her heart hammering in her chest, and pushed the heavy wooden door just enough to peer into the grand ballroom. The flickering candlelight from within seemed to beckon her, a faint warmth against the chill of the late autumn night. The scent of jasmine mingled with the sharp tang of expensive wine, and for a moment, Ivy hesitated, unsure whether to step forward or retreat into the shadows.

Her fingers tightened around the folds of her cloak, the fabric an imperfect shield against the unsettling energy that clung to the place. This was no ordinary event. The invitation itself had been a mystery, sent under the guise of an anonymous benefactor, sealed with a red wax emblem she had never seen before. There had been no mention of the host, no instructions, only a single line of elegant script: Come, if you dare. The words had gnawed at her for days, stirring something deep inside her—a restless curiosity, an undeniable pull toward something dark and unknown.

Her gaze flicked over the polished marble floors of the ballroom, where figures in elegant gowns and sharp tuxedos glided effortlessly across the space. Masked faces turned toward one another in whispered conversations, their voices low and enigmatic. Ivy could feel the weight of their eyes on her, though none turned to acknowledge her directly. It was as though she were a mere shadow among the living, an observer in a world where she did not belong.

But there, standing by the farthest wall, was a figure that drew Ivy's attention in a way nothing else could. He was tall, impossibly so, with a presence that seemed to darken the very air around him. His dark suit was impeccable, tailored to perfection, yet it was his face that captivated Ivy. Strong jawline, high cheekbones, lips set in a faint but knowing curve. His mask, black and intricately adorned with silver filigree, only seemed to enhance the mystery surrounding him. His eyes, though hidden behind the mask, seemed to be watching her—studying her.

Her pulse quickened as their gazes met across the room. She couldn't explain it, but in that instant, it was as if the entire ballroom had fallen away, leaving only the two of them in a suspended, electric moment of tension. His lips parted slightly, as if he were about to speak, but before he could utter a word, the sound of laughter cut through the silence like a blade. Ivy blinked, shaking her head as the spell of his gaze broke, and she realized she had been staring at him for far too long.

Torn between the strange allure of the man and the instinct to leave the room before she did something foolish, Ivy turned to slip back into the shadows of the hallway. But just as she moved, a voice—low and smooth as velvet—reached her ears, sending a shiver down her spine.

"Leaving so soon?"

Ivy froze, her body tense, her breath coming in shallow bursts. She didn't need to turn around to know who had spoken. That voice, as smooth and dangerous as it was, could only belong to him—the man who had been watching her from across the room. He was standing behind her now, too close for comfort, though she hadn't heard his footsteps approach.

"I..." Ivy began, but her throat went dry. She couldn't find the words. She wasn't even sure why she had come here in the first place. Everything about this evening was wrong, yet she couldn't bring herself to leave. Something—no, someone— had called to her, and she had followed without question. It was madness, she knew that.

His shadow fell over her, and she felt the heat of his proximity even through the layers of her cloak. The way he looked at her made her skin flush despite herself. "You're wondering why you were invited," he said, his voice now a quiet murmur, barely audible beneath the hum of conversation that filled the ballroom.

Ivy swallowed, fighting to keep her composure. "I... I don't know," she whispered, the words tasting foreign on her tongue.

"Curiosity can be a dangerous thing," he replied, his tone laced with a warning, though the smirk on his lips suggested he found her hesitation amusing.

She could feel his presence like a weight against her back, pressing her forward, coaxing her to turn around and face him fully. But she resisted, keeping her eyes trained ahead, afraid that if she looked at him too long, she might lose herself entirely in the strange magnetism he exuded.

"What do you want?" she managed, her voice barely a breath.

He was silent for a moment, and Ivy could feel his eyes on her, as though he were studying every inch of her. "I want nothing," he said finally, his voice rich with something she couldn't quite place. "Except for you to stay."

The words sent a ripple through her chest, a pulse of warmth that spread to the tips of her fingers. She turned then, unable to resist the pull any longer. And as she did, his eyes locked onto hers with an intensity that stole the air from her lungs.

"I don't belong here," Ivy said, the truth of her words both painful and undeniable.

"You're wrong," he murmured, his voice softer now, coaxing. "This place was made for you."

Ivy felt the words slide into her veins like fire, igniting something she couldn't name. Something in his eyes, something in the way he stood before her, made it clear: He was no stranger to the shadows, and neither, it seemed, was she. The world around her swirled into a blur of light and music, but all she could focus on was the man before her—the man who, in a single glance, had set her soul on fire.

And somewhere in the distance, a clock struck midnight.

2

A Dangerous Attraction

Ivy's heart raced, her body instinctively wanting to flee from the man who stood too close, his presence like an anchor pulling her into dangerous waters. His gaze was unwavering, steady, as if he could see straight through her, down into the places she had long buried. The air around them felt thick, almost suffocating, as if the room itself held its breath, waiting for something—anything—to happen.

"You've yet to introduce yourself," he said, his voice still a low, mesmerizing drawl. There was a playful undertone to his words, but it was sharp, like a knife hidden beneath silk.

She opened her mouth, but the words caught in her throat. She had expected to be just another unnoticed face in a sea of masked strangers, but somehow, this man had seen her. Not just her appearance, but something deeper, something raw and unguarded. She could feel the pull of his gaze like an invisible thread wrapped around her chest, tightening with each passing second.

"I... I wasn't planning to stay long," she said, her voice unsteady, betraying her calm exterior.

His lips curled into a smile, the kind that didn't reach his eyes. "And yet, here you are. Standing at the edge of something you can't quite resist." His gaze dropped to the hand that still gripped her cloak tightly, as if afraid to let go. "What is it, I wonder? What draws you in, even when every instinct should tell you to run?"

Ivy's pulse quickened. She didn't know how to answer. It wasn't the masked ball, nor the mystery of the invitation that had led her here. It wasn't even the haunting beauty of the room, filled with strangers who moved like ghosts under the flickering candlelight. No, it was him. It was the dark, dangerous energy that seemed to emanate from him, as if he were the very embodiment of the shadows lurking in the corners of the room.

"I should go," Ivy said again, her words barely audible now. She knew that turning away was the only safe option, the only way to escape the suffocating pull he seemed to have on her.

But he took a step forward, closing the distance between them, and for a moment, Ivy thought her heart might stop. His proximity was overwhelming, and yet, she couldn't move, as though his very presence had rooted her to the floor.

"Tell me your name," he murmured, his breath warm against her ear. "I'll let you leave when you tell me your name."

Ivy felt her knees weaken, her entire body betraying her as she found herself caught in the web of his quiet insistence. There was something hypnotic about the way he spoke, as though his voice was a thread that wound around her, pulling her deeper into his world. But she couldn't. She had to resist. She had to protect herself.

"I don't think you'd want to know," she managed to say, her voice thick with a mixture of fear and longing. She didn't trust herself. She didn't trust him.

A soft laugh escaped him, though it wasn't entirely amused. "You're more intriguing than I thought." He took another step, and this time, Ivy felt his fingers brush against the edge of her cloak, sending a ripple of heat through her skin. The touch was brief but electrifying, and it left a mark on her, one she couldn't erase.

"I think you're lying," he said, his eyes never leaving hers. "You do want me to know your name, Ivy."

Her breath hitched, and she staggered back, her cloak slipping slightly from her shoulders in the motion. How did he—? How could he possibly know? She hadn't told anyone her name since she'd arrived, and yet he seemed to have the power to unearth every secret she thought was buried deep inside her.

"Who are you?" she whispered, her voice trembling now with a mix of fear and fascination. "Why are you doing this?"

His expression darkened, and for a moment, Ivy thought she

saw something else in his eyes—something colder, sharper. But it was gone in an instant, replaced by that same unreadable gaze that made her feel both exposed and protected at the same time.

"Because you're here," he said simply, his tone devoid of emotion. "And you're not meant to be here, are you, Ivy?"

She took a step back, her mind scrambling for a way to escape, but her body refused to cooperate. There was nowhere to run, nowhere to hide from him, and that terrified her. But even as fear coiled inside her chest, she couldn't deny the strange, magnetic pull he had on her. It was as if the very essence of who he was called to something deep within her—something she didn't understand, but couldn't ignore.

"Why do you say that?" Ivy managed, her voice barely above a whisper. She was desperate now, trying to regain control, to make sense of the growing unease that gnawed at her insides.

His lips twisted into something almost like a smile, but it was a smile that promised nothing good. "Because, Ivy, you've stepped into a world you don't understand. And now, there's no going back."

The weight of his words settled over her like a heavy cloak, and Ivy realized, with a sinking feeling in her gut, that she had just walked into something far darker than she could ever have imagined.

Before she could say anything more, the sound of a bell rang out, sharp and clear, cutting through the tension in the room like a blade. Ivy's eyes darted to the clock above the fireplace, and for a fleeting moment, she was certain it hadn't been there before.

The man's gaze followed hers, his expression unreadable. Then, without another word, he turned and walked away, his figure disappearing into the shadows of the ballroom as if he were nothing more than a ghost.

Ivy stood frozen, her thoughts racing. What had just happened? Had it all been a game? A trap? Or something far more dangerous than she could ever comprehend?

She didn't know, but one thing was certain: She wasn't leaving now. She couldn't. Not when the danger had just begun to unfold.

3

The Burning Touch

The question hung in the air like smoke, curling around Ivy's thoughts, thick and suffocating. Who was he? The man before her—this stranger with the eyes that seemed to pierce into her very soul—had left her speechless, his presence as undeniable as the shadows that seemed to cling to him. Her pulse throbbed in her temples as she tried to make sense of the situation, tried to find some foothold in the disorienting rush of emotions that swirled inside her.

"I told you," he murmured, his voice low and dark, like the rumble of distant thunder. "You know exactly who I am."

Ivy's chest tightened. It wasn't that she knew him—not really—but somehow, she felt as though she had always known him, as though their paths were somehow fated to cross. His name, or the idea of his name, hovered just beyond her grasp, like a word she had forgotten the meaning of. There was no explanation for the sense of familiarity that stirred within her, nor the strange compulsion to step closer, despite every logical instinct screaming at her to run.

She opened her mouth to protest, to demand more, but before she could speak, the world around them seemed to shift. The sound of muffled laughter and the clinking of glasses faded into a dull hum, the edges of her vision blurring as she became acutely aware of the heat that radiated from his body. His proximity was intoxicating—overwhelming—and yet, Ivy couldn't step away. She couldn't look away.

The moment stretched on, taut and fragile, until finally, his hand reached out, brushing against her arm. The touch was light, feather-soft, but it felt like fire. Her breath caught in her throat, her pulse erratic as an electric current shot through her veins. She froze, eyes wide, as the world around her seemed to close in. His fingers lingered for a heartbeat longer than necessary, the warmth from his touch sinking deep into her skin, igniting something inside her that she didn't understand.

"I've been waiting for you," he said, his voice barely more than a whisper now, but the words reverberated through her body, leaving her disoriented and breathless.

She recoiled, the grip on her cloak tightening as though it could shield her from the intensity of what she felt. But she knew it wasn't just the touch that had shaken her—it was him, all of him. The way he looked at her, the way his presence wrapped around her like a storm she couldn't escape. It was as though the world had become an entirely different place, with the two of them standing at the center, caught in some dangerous dance she wasn't sure she wanted to be a part of.

"I don't understand," she said, her voice trembling despite her best efforts to sound calm. "Why are you doing this?"

His smile deepened, that same knowing, dangerous smile, and for a moment, she wondered if she had made a terrible mistake by coming here. But it was too late for second thoughts; she was already tangled in this web, already ensnared by him. She could feel it, a heavy weight settling over her heart, and in that moment, Ivy realized that the moment she stepped into this house, this cursed mansion, she had signed some unspoken pact. There was no going back.

"I could tell you," he said, his voice dropping even lower, "but where would be the fun in that?"

The way he said it, the playful, mocking tone, made her stomach flip. Ivy hated that part of her that wanted to stay, wanted to know more. Her mind screamed at her to be smart, to leave, but her body felt like it was made of something molten, like she might melt right into the floor if she didn't move.

His hand shifted then, brushing a stray lock of hair from her face, the touch so tender it almost felt like a lie. She stared at him, her lips parted, unsure of what to do, how to react. Every nerve in her body was alive, her senses heightened in a way that felt both exhilarating and terrifying.

"I think you've come here for a reason," he continued, his voice almost hypnotic now. "Maybe you didn't know it, but I think you've been searching for something." His gaze hardened, darkening like a storm cloud just before it bursts. "And I'm afraid you've found it."

Ivy's chest constricted as a shiver ran down her spine. His words felt like a warning, but they also felt like a promise— a promise that whatever this was between them, it wasn't just a fleeting encounter. It was something more. Something dangerous.

"I—I don't want any part of this," Ivy whispered, the words sounding weak even to her own ears.

But his smile only deepened, that cold, dangerous smile that made her heart skip a beat.

"You've already made your choice, Ivy. And it's too late to walk away now."

With that, he stepped back, his gaze never leaving hers as he slowly disappeared into the crowd. The ballroom, once filled with vibrant life, seemed suddenly alien to Ivy, as though the ground had shifted beneath her feet. The air was thick with unspoken promises and hidden dangers, and she was standing at the center of it all, her heart beating faster with every passing second.

In that moment, Ivy realized she was already burned. And whatever happened next, she wouldn't be able to escape.

$$4$$

Ghosts of the Past

The air in the ballroom had thickened, charged with an almost suffocating intensity. Ivy could feel the weight of every eye on her, though none of the guests dared look directly at her. It was as though they were all waiting for something, but none dared to speak. She was acutely aware of the stranger's presence, still so close, his every breath a sound she felt more than heard. His touch lingered on her arm, his fingers tracing a path she couldn't quite follow, and every nerve in her body screamed for her to pull away, to run, to do anything but stay.

But she couldn't. She was rooted to the spot, entranced by him, or perhaps by the storm he brought with him.

His gaze never wavered as it held hers, an unspoken challenge in his eyes. She knew, somehow, that he was waiting for her to make the next move. Waiting for her to step deeper into the web he had woven with every word, every glance, every touch. She was terrified, but also, inexplicably, drawn to him, as if she had been walking toward this moment all her life.

"Ivy," he said, the sound of her name rolling off his tongue with a smoothness that made her insides twist. "You've been curious about me, haven't you?"

She swallowed hard, her throat dry, unsure how to respond. The questions had been gnawing at her since the moment she received the mysterious invitation, but hearing him say it aloud—his certainty that she had been watching him, studying him—it unsettled her more than she cared to admit.

"I..." Her voice faltered. She hadn't come here to flirt or indulge in whatever game he was playing. She had come for answers, for something she couldn't quite name but knew she had to find.

"You didn't expect this," he continued, his voice dipping lower. There was a trace of something almost predatory in his tone, a satisfaction in knowing he had the upper hand. "You thought you'd remain a stranger in the crowd, blending in with the others." He took a step closer, his face now inches from hers, his breath warm on her skin. "But you're not like them, are you, Ivy?"

Her heart slammed against her ribs. She didn't know what he meant, but something inside her—the part of her that had come here against all sense, the part that was somehow more alive than ever before—knew that she couldn't back down. Not now. Not with the way he was looking at her, like he knew exactly what she needed, even if she didn't.

"I don't belong here," she managed to whisper, more to herself than to him. "I shouldn't be here."

A smile tugged at the corners of his lips, but it wasn't comforting. It wasn't reassuring. It was the smile of someone who knew the dark corners of the world, who had seen things others couldn't even begin to imagine.

"No," he said softly, almost tenderly. "You shouldn't."

The words settled over her like a cold shroud, but before she could react, his hand slid gently to her wrist, his touch burning through the fabric of her sleeve. She stiffened, her breath catching in her throat as a flood of memories surged in from the depths of her mind.

A shadow passed across the room, momentarily breaking their connection, and for just a split second, Ivy thought she saw something in his eyes—something unfamiliar, something painful. But it was gone before she could fully comprehend it, swallowed by the same darkness that clung to him. It was a fleeting moment, barely perceptible, but it sent a ripple through her, as though she had caught a glimpse of a ghost from his past.

"Ivy," he said again, his voice now firm, compelling her attention. "I want to show you something."

The words sent a shiver down her spine, but she couldn't bring herself to resist. She didn't want to resist. For some inexplicable reason, she trusted him. No, not trust—she needed him, needed whatever it was he had to offer, no matter how dangerous it might be.

He led her away from the crowd, his grip on her wrist gentle but insistent. They moved through the crowd of masked figures like a current in a river, unnoticed by all but a few, who watched them with an unsettling intensity. It was as if they knew what was coming, as if they had been waiting for it.

They ascended a grand staircase, the ornate ironwork creaking under their weight, and Ivy felt a tremor in the pit of her stomach as they reached the second floor. The corridor stretched before them, lined with portraits of men and women whose faces seemed too still, too lifelike—almost as if they were watching her.

Without a word, he stopped in front of a door at the end of the hall. The door was old, its wood darkened with age, and the brass handle gleamed faintly in the dim light of the hallway.

"This is where the past waits for you," he murmured, and with a single twist of his wrist, the door creaked open.

Ivy's pulse quickened. She didn't know what to expect, but she knew one thing: whatever lay beyond that door would change everything.

5

Ashes and Betrayal

Ivy couldn't breathe. Every fiber of her being screamed at her to pull away, to run, to tear herself from the man who held her in a grip she could neither resist nor understand. His hand was still wrapped around her wrist, but it wasn't just the physical touch that bound her—it was the overwhelming force of his presence, the unspoken weight of the words he hadn't said but that she could feel vibrating in the air between them.

"Where are you taking me?" Ivy whispered, her voice barely audible, almost lost in the hum of the distant music from the ballroom. It sounded miles away, as if the space around them had thickened and compressed, leaving them both trapped in a void of their own making.

"Somewhere no one will find us," he replied, his voice smooth and dark, like a promise wrapped in silk. There was something about the way he spoke, a quiet, dangerous confidence that made her pulse quicken, despite her every instinct to turn and flee.

Her heart pounded in her chest, and the room seemed to close in around her, the walls pressing in with an oppressive, suffocating pressure. She had come here with questions—so many questions—but now, with every step they took away from the ball and deeper into the mansion, Ivy wasn't sure she wanted the answers. Not anymore. The man at her side, the one who claimed to know her name before she even said it, had a dark gravity about him. It was as though he was pulling her into a storm, and no matter how hard she tried to resist, she knew she wouldn't be able to stop it.

They moved down a narrow hallway, the heavy scent of wood and dust thick in the air. Ivy stumbled, her heels echoing against the marble floors as she tried to keep pace with him. The corridor stretched on, dimly lit by a few flickering sconces, and with each passing step, the atmosphere seemed to grow colder, darker. Her breath began to come in short bursts, and the tension in her shoulders made them ache. She could feel the weight of his eyes on her, could sense his every movement beside her, as though he were some kind of shadow, a presence that had always existed just beyond the reach of her understanding.

He stopped in front of a door at the end of the hallway, his hand pressing gently against the handle. Ivy couldn't see what lay beyond it, but she felt an unmistakable sense of dread creep over her skin. It was as though everything inside her, every instinct, was telling her not to go through that door—not to trust whatever was waiting on the other side. But before she could voice the protest building in her throat, he pushed the door open, the sound of it creaking loudly in the stillness of the house.

The room beyond was nothing like the grand ballroom they had left behind. It was small, the walls lined with bookshelves that stretched to the high ceiling, filled with books that looked as though they hadn't been touched in years. A single desk sat in the center of the room, papers scattered across its surface. And in the far corner, a large, ornate mirror stood—tarnished, the glass cracked, as if it had been deliberately damaged. But it wasn't the room that caught Ivy's attention. It was the strange, oppressive feeling that lingered in the air, as though the room itself was holding its breath, waiting for something.

"Sit," the man commanded softly, his voice low, carrying an authority that left no room for argument.

Ivy hesitated, glancing around the room as if looking for an escape, though she knew she wouldn't find one. His grip on her wrist tightened, pulling her toward the desk. The papers on it were a jumble—scribbled notes, half-finished letters, and what looked like a map, though the ink was blurred, smeared with age. She didn't want to sit. She didn't want to stay in this room with him. But the moment she felt his fingers leave her wrist, the unease inside her seemed to surge like a wave, and she slowly, reluctantly, sank into the chair he had gestured to.

The door shut behind him with a finality that seemed to reverberate in the pit of her stomach. For a long moment, neither of them spoke. Ivy couldn't understand why she was still here, why she hadn't run the moment she had the chance. She knew something was wrong—knew that this was no accident, no chance encounter—but there was no easy way out now. The trap had already been set.

He stood by the desk, his back turned, staring down at the scattered papers. The silence stretched on, heavy and suffocating. Ivy opened her mouth to speak, to ask again who he was, but the words caught in her throat.

Finally, he spoke, his voice dark and filled with an edge she hadn't heard before.

"You've heard of my family, haven't you?"

His words hit her like a slap. Ivy's heart skipped a beat, her throat tightening. The Ashford family. The name rang in her head like an echo of something long buried. She had heard whispers, rumors—the kind of things you only heard in passing, in hushed tones, in the corners of a room where no one dared to speak too loudly. The Ashfords were known for their wealth, their power, but also for the shadows that surrounded them. Secrets. Betrayals. Scandals that no one dared to speak of, except in the most private of conversations.

"I know the name," Ivy said, her voice shaking despite her efforts to sound composed. "But I don't know why…"

"Why I brought you here?" His voice was soft, almost mocking now, as he turned to face her, his eyes gleaming with something dangerous, something wild. "Because, Ivy, you've always known. You just never wanted to believe it."

His words cut through her like a blade. She had no idea what he meant. What was he talking about? But before she could respond, he continued, his gaze cold, calculating.

"The man you think you know—the one you came here to find—doesn't exist. Not in the way you think." His eyes narrowed, a flicker of something darker passing through them. "Your questions, your curiosity... They've led you straight to the heart of a betrayal."

Ivy's stomach dropped. The words hung in the air like a death sentence, and the world around her seemed to blur as her thoughts raced. Betrayal. Her mind couldn't wrap around it. She had come here for answers, for some sense of clarity, but all she had found was more darkness, more questions. The man before her—this Ashford—was a riddle, one she had no hope of solving. And she was only beginning to understand the depth of the game she had stepped into.

6

The Whispering Shadows

The letter trembled in Ivy's hands, but it wasn't from the cold. It was from something far deeper, something darker that had settled into the very marrow of her bones. The words on the page seemed to grow heavier with every heartbeat, pressing in on her, suffocating her. She could feel the air around her thickening, the room closing in as though the walls themselves were conspiring to swallow her whole. Her breath came in shallow bursts, but she couldn't look away from the man who stood before her, the architect of this twisted dance they were now caught in.

"You're not surprised, are you?" he asked softly, his voice like silk over broken glass. "No, I can see it in your eyes. You've always known, haven't you?"

Ivy's throat tightened, her words trapped by the sudden weight of his gaze. It wasn't a question—at least, not one she could answer. She didn't know what she knew anymore. She didn't know what to believe. The strange pull he had on her, the way he seemed to see into her soul, made her wonder if this was all part of something larger, something beyond her control. Perhaps she had never been in control at all.

The letter crumpled in her hand as she clenched her fist around it, the paper now a mere symbol of the turmoil tearing through her.

"You've come too far to turn back now," he continued, his voice low, almost comforting in its familiarity. "I can see it in you, Ivy. The way you're trembling, the way you're trying to make sense of everything. You feel it, don't you? The weight of it. The danger."

Her pulse raced at the mention of danger, though she could not say whether it was the danger of the unknown or the danger that lay in the man himself that terrified her more. She couldn't understand why her feet felt rooted to the floor, why her mind was so full of questions that no one could answer. But she was afraid. Afraid of him, afraid of the shadows that seemed to pulse with life, and afraid of what might happen if she let herself fall into the madness she could feel swirling around them both.

"What is this?" Ivy whispered, her voice trembling with the weight of a thousand unasked questions. "What do you want from me?"

He stepped closer, the faintest of smiles curling at the corners of his lips. His presence filled the room in a way that felt suffocating, as though his very existence was larger than the space they stood in. She tried to move back, but her legs felt weak, her body too heavy to obey her.

"I don't want anything from you, Ivy," he said, his tone so calm it was almost unsettling. "Not anymore. But you..." He paused, as if savoring the moment. "You want everything, don't you?"

The way he said it sent a shiver down her spine. She couldn't deny it—there was a hunger inside her, a gnawing need to understand, to know the truth, even if that truth was something she wasn't sure she could handle.

"Stop," she breathed, her chest rising and falling in ragged gasps. "Just... stop."

The room seemed to pulse with the force of her words, as though the very air was thickening, turning to something darker, something malevolent. She closed her eyes, trying to force the image of him from her mind, trying to erase the feeling of his touch, his gaze, the very pull of his presence. But it was impossible. His shadow lingered over her, casting itself over her thoughts, her heart, and her every breath.

And then, in the quietest of whispers, she heard it.

A voice. Soft, like the rustle of leaves in a dark forest, whispering from the very depths of the room. Ivy's eyes snapped open, her pulse thundering in her ears. The man had not moved. His expression had not shifted. But the voice was still there, a low murmur that seemed to come from all around them.

"Ivy," it whispered, "you can't escape. No one can."

The voice seemed to echo in her mind, wrapping itself around her like tendrils of smoke. Her head snapped back, her gaze darting around the room, searching for the source, but there was nothing—only shadows that seemed to move and breathe in the dim light.

She spun back toward the man, her hands shaking as the crumpled letter fell from her grip, scattering to the floor. "What is happening? What is that voice?" Her breath was shallow, desperate.

The man didn't answer at first. He just stood there, his face unreadable, watching her with that same, inscrutable gaze. She hated that look. It was the look of someone who knew things that she didn't, and no matter how hard she tried, she couldn't break through it.

"That," he finally said, his voice almost too calm, "is the voice of your past. The past you thought you had escaped." He stepped closer, his gaze never leaving her, his presence a suffocating weight. "That voice... is the reason you're here. The reason you came."

Ivy shook her head violently, trying to push the words away. The past. She had thought she had left it behind. She had thought the nightmares were gone, buried under layers of time and distance. But now, the truth was dawning on her, a realization that was as sharp and painful as a wound.

She looked at him, her eyes wide with terror. "What have I done?" she whispered.

The shadows in the room seemed to stir, as if they had a life of their own, breathing in time with her panicked thoughts.

And then, she understood.

The truth was never what it seemed, and the ghosts of the past were never truly gone. They were waiting. Watching. And now, they had come to claim her.

7

The Whispering Shadows

The letter trembled in Ivy's hands, but it wasn't from the cold. It was from something far deeper, something darker that had settled into the very marrow of her bones. The words on the page seemed to grow heavier with every heartbeat, pressing in on her, suffocating her. She could feel the air around her thickening, the room closing in as though the walls themselves were conspiring to swallow her whole. Her breath came in shallow bursts, but she couldn't look away from the man who stood before her, the architect of this twisted dance they were now caught in.

"You're not surprised, are you?" he asked softly, his voice like silk over broken glass. "No, I can see it in your eyes. You've always known, haven't you?"

Ivy's throat tightened, her words trapped by the sudden weight of his gaze. It wasn't a question—at least, not one she could answer. She didn't know what she knew anymore. She didn't know what to believe. The strange pull he had on her, the way he seemed to see into her soul, made her wonder if this was all part of something larger, something beyond her control. Perhaps she had never been in control at all.

The letter crumpled in her hand as she clenched her fist around it, the paper now a mere symbol of the turmoil tearing through her.

"You've come too far to turn back now," he continued, his voice low, almost comforting in its familiarity. "I can see it in you, Ivy. The way you're trembling, the way you're trying to make sense of everything. You feel it, don't you? The weight of it. The danger."

Her pulse raced at the mention of danger, though she could not say whether it was the danger of the unknown or the danger that lay in the man himself that terrified her more. She couldn't understand why her feet felt rooted to the floor, why her mind was so full of questions that no one could answer. But she was afraid. Afraid of him, afraid of the shadows that seemed to pulse with life, and afraid of what might happen if she let herself fall into the madness she could feel swirling around them both.

"What is this?" Ivy whispered, her voice trembling with the weight of a thousand unasked questions. "What do you want from me?"

He stepped closer, the faintest of smiles curling at the corners of his lips. His presence filled the room in a way that felt suffocating, as though his very existence was larger than the space they stood in. She tried to move back, but her legs felt weak, her body too heavy to obey her.

"I don't want anything from you, Ivy," he said, his tone so calm it was almost unsettling. "Not anymore. But you..." He paused, as if savoring the moment. "You want everything, don't you?"

The way he said it sent a shiver down her spine. She couldn't deny it—there was a hunger inside her, a gnawing need to understand, to know the truth, even if that truth was something she wasn't sure she could handle.

"Stop," she breathed, her chest rising and falling in ragged gasps. "Just... stop."

The room seemed to pulse with the force of her words, as though the very air was thickening, turning to something darker, something malevolent. She closed her eyes, trying to force the image of him from her mind, trying to erase the feeling of his touch, his gaze, the very pull of his presence. But it was impossible. His shadow lingered over her, casting itself over her thoughts, her heart, and her every breath.

And then, in the quietest of whispers, she heard it.

A voice. Soft, like the rustle of leaves in a dark forest, whispering from the very depths of the room. Ivy's eyes snapped open, her pulse thundering in her ears. The man had not moved. His expression had not shifted. But the voice was still there, a low murmur that seemed to come from all around them.

"Ivy," it whispered, "you can't escape. No one can."

The voice seemed to echo in her mind, wrapping itself around her like tendrils of smoke. Her head snapped back, her gaze darting around the room, searching for the source, but there was nothing—only shadows that seemed to move and breathe in the dim light.

She spun back toward the man, her hands shaking as the crumpled letter fell from her grip, scattering to the floor. "What is happening? What is that voice?" Her breath was shallow, desperate.

The man didn't answer at first. He just stood there, his face unreadable, watching her with that same, inscrutable gaze. She hated that look. It was the look of someone who knew things that she didn't, and no matter how hard she tried, she couldn't break through it.

"That," he finally said, his voice almost too calm, "is the voice of your past. The past you thought you had escaped." He stepped closer, his gaze never leaving her, his presence a suffocating weight. "That voice... is the reason you're here. The reason you came."

Ivy shook her head violently, trying to push the words away. The past. She had thought she had left it behind. She had thought the nightmares were gone, buried under layers of time and distance. But now, the truth was dawning on her, a realization that was as sharp and painful as a wound.

She looked at him, her eyes wide with terror. "What have I done?" she whispered.

The shadows in the room seemed to stir, as if they had a life of their own, breathing in time with her panicked thoughts.

And then, she understood.

The truth was never what it seemed, and the ghosts of the past were never truly gone. They were waiting. Watching. And now, they had come to claim her.

8

The Echo of Forgotten Voices

The voice was faint at first, like a ripple in the air, barely audible. But it wasn't just in her ears—it was in her bones, deep inside her. It reverberated through the space, a soft whisper that seemed to come from every direction, slipping through the cracks of the mansion like a secret too dangerous to be spoken aloud. Ivy froze, her body stiffening, her eyes scanning the room as though she might find the source of the voice, though she knew deep down it wasn't something that could be seen.

"Do not listen to him."

The words came again, a faint murmur in the oppressive silence that had swallowed the room whole. This time, the voice was clearer, sharper, as though it had crossed a threshold and was now fully awake. Ivy's breath caught in her throat, and she looked frantically around the room, but all she saw was the man standing just a few paces away, his gaze fixed on her with an intensity that made her skin crawl.

"You hear it, don't you?" His voice cut through her panic like a blade, his words threading through the air with the precision of a predator cornering its prey. "You're listening to the shadows now, aren't you? I told you, Ivy, you don't know what you're dealing with."

Ivy's heart hammered in her chest, her hand gripping the edge of the desk for support. She hadn't imagined it. She couldn't have. The voice was real, tangible, and it had spoken to her—directly to her. It wasn't the man. It wasn't him who had whispered those words, that warning. But who, then?

Her gaze darted to the cracked mirror in the corner of the room, its surface reflecting nothing but darkness, a void that seemed to swallow the light. There was something about the mirror, something that pulled at her, tugged at the corners of her mind, urging her to look closer, to understand what lay beyond it.

She took a cautious step forward, but the man's hand shot out, grabbing her arm with an iron grip that sent a shock through her body. His touch burned, but not in the way it had before. This time, it was colder, like ice seeping into her very skin, freezing her blood.

"Don't go near it," he said, his voice low and dangerous, the warning in his tone unmistakable. "You're not ready to see it."

But the voice in her head—the voice that had spoken from the depths of the room—was louder now, insistent. Go to the mirror. Look into the glass.

Her body moved on its own, her feet carrying her toward the mirror despite the man's warning, despite the growing terror that gnawed at her insides. She had to see. She had to understand. The voice was right, wasn't it? She wasn't ready for this, but somehow, she knew she was already too far gone. The moment she stepped into this place, she had sealed her fate. There was no turning back.

The man let out a curse, his fingers tightening around her wrist in a desperate attempt to stop her, but Ivy wrenched herself free, her pulse racing as she approached the mirror. She could feel the coldness radiating from its surface, a chill that made her skin crawl. The glass was cracked, the fractures running through it like veins of darkness, but as she drew closer, she could swear she saw something moving inside the reflection.

A figure. Dark, blurry, but unmistakably there.

Her breath caught in her throat, and for a moment, she almost stumbled back, but her feet refused to obey. The reflection in the mirror began to clear, and Ivy's blood ran cold as the shape in the glass took form.

It was her. But it wasn't.

The reflection that stared back at her was twisted, distorted, like a ghostly version of herself. Her face was pale, her eyes hollow, like something was draining the life from her. But there was more. Behind her, in the shadows of the mirror, stood something darker—something that wasn't there in the room. A figure that was too tall, too still, with eyes that glowed like embers in the dark.

She gasped, stumbling back, but her feet felt like lead, and she couldn't pull herself away. The figure in the mirror moved toward her, its presence so overwhelming that she felt suffocated by it, as if the very air had turned to smoke.

"I told you," the voice whispered again, the one that had come from the shadows, "you're already too far gone. There's no escape from what you've seen."

The man was behind her now, his breath hot against her neck, but it was the reflection in the mirror that held her captive. The dark figure reached out, its fingers stretching toward her, impossibly long, the nails like claws, and Ivy knew—knew—that it wasn't just a reflection. It was something else, something that had always been there, watching her.

And just as the figure's fingers brushed against the glass, the mirror shattered with a deafening crack.

Shards of glass flew through the air, and Ivy screamed, her mind spinning with fear and confusion. The room seemed to tilt, the walls spinning, and the floor dropped away beneath her feet. She reached out, desperate to grab onto something, anything, to steady herself. But before she could, everything went black.

When Ivy woke, she was no longer in the room. The mirror was gone, replaced by a strange, cold darkness that stretched out in every direction. The voice whispered again, but this time, it was not the voice of a warning. It was a voice of promise.

The path has been set. Welcome to the beginning, Ivy.

9

The Weight of the Hollow Mirror

Ivy's breath came in shallow, ragged gasps as she stood frozen before the mirror. The reflection that stared back at her was no longer her own, not in any way she recognized. The image was distorted, warped like something that had been torn from a nightmare. Her eyes were hollow, dark pits where her irises should have been, and her skin—her skin was ashen, drained of all color, like the lifeless surface of a corpse.

The reflection moved, but not in sync with her own body. It tilted its head to one side, a sickly smile stretching across its face—her face—though Ivy could feel the bile rise in her throat at the sheer wrongness of it. The figure in the mirror didn't belong to her. It was as if the mirror had stolen her essence, twisted it into something cruel and mocking.

She reached out a hand instinctively, her fingers trembling, but the reflection in the glass did the same. For a split second, Ivy thought she might touch the cold surface of the glass and find some kind of connection, but her fingers went straight through the reflection as though it were nothing but vapor. Her pulse raced, panic surging within her. The hollow eyes of the figure stared back at her, and for a fleeting moment, Ivy could have sworn it wasn't her own fear she saw in them—it was something darker, something ancient, something that had been waiting.

The chill in the air thickened, spreading across her skin in a crawling, suffocating wave. Her chest tightened, the weight of an invisible hand pressing down on her. She wanted to look away, to tear her gaze from the mirror, but she couldn't. Something held her there, something invisible but powerful, like an unspoken command.

"Don't move," a voice whispered behind her. The man's voice.

She whirled around, her heart racing, but when she saw him standing there, just a few feet away, the words didn't feel like a warning—they felt like a threat. His eyes locked onto hers, his gaze cold and distant, like a predator watching its prey.

"I told you to stay away from it," he said again, his voice low, dangerously calm. "You don't know what it can do. You don't understand what you're looking at."

Ivy opened her mouth to speak, to ask him what the hell was happening, but the words caught in her throat. She didn't know if she was more terrified of the man or of the reflection that seemed to mock her very existence. She wanted to turn away, to run, but her feet felt as though they were cemented to the floor. The mirror called to her. It knew her, knew her fears, her weaknesses, her desires. It whispered her name, a soft sound that seemed to come from the walls themselves, from the very heart of the mansion.

"You don't belong here," the figure in the mirror said, its lips curling into that same twisted smile. The voice was wrong, so wrong—like the echo of something that had been lost to time. "You never did."

Ivy staggered backward, her hands shooting out to catch the desk for support, but the air around her felt thick, oppressive. The man had stepped closer, his shadow falling across her as his gaze never left her face. She could feel the heat of him, the weight of his presence like an iron hand gripping her chest, choking the air from her lungs.

"No," she whispered, her voice barely audible. "What is it? What do you want from me?"

He didn't answer right away, and in that moment, the silence in the room seemed to stretch on forever, thick and suffocating. The only sound was the beating of her own heart, so loud in her ears it felt like it might burst from her chest.

"You should never have come here, Ivy," the man finally said, his voice so soft, so laced with something almost... tender. "But now that you're here, there's no turning back. You're part of it now. You've always been part of it."

Ivy shook her head, unable to process what he was saying. She couldn't breathe. She felt as though the walls of the room were closing in on her, the edges of her vision darkening.

"Look again," he urged, his voice almost a command. "Look into the mirror, Ivy. And see what's waiting."

Her hands shook violently as she turned back to the glass. The reflection in the mirror had changed again, the figure now standing at the edge of the frame, its distorted face a mere shadow, the hollow eyes fixed on hers. It moved toward her, its movements unnatural, jerking as though it were tethered to some unseen force.

The room seemed to spin, and Ivy's head swam with dizziness. The whispering started again, low at first, like the murmuring of voices behind closed doors. The figure in the glass opened its mouth, and the words that came out were not human. It was an ancient language, the sounds alien and guttural, like the growl of something long buried, long forgotten.

As the last syllable fell from its mouth, the air around Ivy went still. She felt the weight of its gaze on her soul, like invisible fingers digging into her very essence. The reflection in the mirror seemed to shimmer for a moment, and then, with a sickening crack, the glass split.

The room darkened as the reflection seemed to reach toward her, the sound of glass splintering filling the air. She couldn't move, couldn't speak. Every instinct in her body screamed at her to run, to escape, but it was too late. The mirror was no longer just a reflection—it was a doorway, and Ivy had just stepped through.

The man's voice cut through the rising tension like a blade. "It's too late for you, Ivy."

And then, the darkness consumed her.

10

The Echoes of Despair

Ivy's heart pounded in her chest as she stared at the man, the air between them thick with an unspoken tension. The reflection in the mirror—her reflection—was still moving, still smiling that terrible, empty smile. She wanted to scream, to shout, to demand answers, but her voice wouldn't come. Her throat was dry, constricted, and the words seemed to die before they could escape her lips.

The man stepped forward, his presence swallowing the room, drowning out everything else. The shadows in the corners seemed to lengthen and twist, creeping toward them like living things, and Ivy felt her pulse spike. There was something about him—something ancient and unfathomable—that made her feel both insignificant and utterly exposed.

His gaze, cold and sharp as ice, never left her. "You think you understand what's happening here, Ivy," he said, his voice low and steady, like a storm on the horizon. "You think you can walk away from this. But you can't. Not anymore. You're already in too deep."

A chill ran down her spine. The words hit her like a slap, like an icy wind against her skin. She wanted to deny it, to say that she could walk away, that she could leave this place and never look back. But deep down, she knew it was a lie. She had crossed a line. And now, there was no going back.

"What are you?" she managed to choke out, her voice trembling. The words felt foreign coming from her, like they didn't belong to her, as if she wasn't even sure she wanted the answer.

The man didn't move, his expression unreadable, but there was a flicker in his eyes—something sharp, something old. "What am I? You think you can understand that? You think you're ready for the truth?"

Ivy felt a sick twist in her stomach, but she couldn't look away. She could feel her body betraying her, pulling her toward him, as if there was some invisible thread that connected them both, binding them together in some twisted dance she couldn't escape.

The mirror flickered again, and her reflection shifted. The smile on her reflection's face was gone now, replaced by something else—a look of recognition. The figure in the glass stared back at her, eyes wide, and Ivy's heart skipped a beat. It wasn't her anymore, not really. This figure wasn't her. It was something else, something darker, something that had been waiting for her to see it, to acknowledge it.

A voice—familiar, but wrong—whispered through her mind. You've always known, Ivy. Always known that you were meant for something more. You never understood it, but now... now you will.

The words echoed in her head, filling her thoughts, drowning out everything else. The room seemed to warp around her, the walls bending inward, the shadows creeping closer, wrapping around her like a suffocating fog. She struggled to breathe, her chest tightening with every passing second. The man moved closer, his presence a suffocating weight that pressed on her from all sides.

"You've been looking for answers," he said, his voice almost gentle now, like a confession. "But the truth is more dangerous than you could ever imagine. It's not something you can control. And you—" He paused, his gaze flicking over her, his eyes dark and cold, like two black holes pulling at her soul. "You're already tangled in it."

The words sent a shiver of dread coursing through Ivy's veins. She didn't want to hear this. She didn't want to believe it. But somewhere deep down, she knew it was true. There was no escaping this place, no escaping him.

"I didn't ask for this," she whispered, almost to herself, her voice cracking with a mix of fear and disbelief.

The man's lips curled into a faint smile, but it wasn't kind. It wasn't reassuring. It was a smile that belonged to someone who knew things she couldn't begin to comprehend. "No," he said softly. "But that's the thing, Ivy. No one ever asks for this."

The shadows behind him seemed to stretch further now, growing darker, thicker, as if the very room was being consumed by something far worse than anything she could see. The mirror flickered again, the surface of the glass rippling like water disturbed by an unseen hand. The figure in the mirror shifted once more, but this time it was different. It stepped forward, its movements slow and deliberate, as if it were walking toward her, through the glass, into the room.

Ivy took a step back, her legs shaking, her breath coming in shallow gasps. She reached out, her hand trembling, as if she could push away the shadows, but they closed in around her, swallowing the light. The reflection in the mirror—the creature that wasn't her but was also her—stepped closer, its eyes locked onto Ivy's, and in that instant, she knew.

She was not alone in this room. Not anymore.

There was something—someone—else. Something far darker than she could ever understand, and it had been waiting for her, for this moment. The figure in the glass reached out its hand toward her, and Ivy felt the pull, like a gravitational force she couldn't fight. The man's cold, dark eyes flickered toward the mirror, then back at Ivy, and for the first time, something close to regret flashed in his gaze.

But it was too late. The reflection was already reaching for her, its fingers inches from her face. The coldness of its touch would consume her whole.

And there was nothing she could do to stop it.

II

Part Two

The Flames of Desire

11

The Court of Ashes

The room seemed to stretch in every direction, the walls whispering as though they were alive, the shadows dancing like forgotten memories. Ivy's legs trembled beneath her, the weight of the moment crashing down on her. She had no idea what had brought her to this point, no comprehension of how everything had spiraled so far out of control. But the man—the figure who stood before her, whose presence had infected the very air—was something she couldn't ignore, something she couldn't outrun.

His gaze locked onto hers, his eyes burning with a cold intensity that made her insides writhe. There was nothing human in them, nothing soft or comforting. They were the eyes of a predator, of something ancient, something far older than the world itself. His presence was like a thick fog that she couldn't escape, filling the room and smothering her every thought.

"You're standing in the Court of Ashes," he said, his voice like the crackle of fire on dry wood, rich with malice. "And you've come too far to turn back now."

Ivy swallowed hard, trying to steady her breathing, but the words echoed in her mind like a death sentence. The Court of Ashes. The name felt like a promise—dark, unyielding, inevitable. The walls around her seemed to shift, the light growing dimmer, as if the room itself were responding to the words. She couldn't tell if it was the flickering of candlelight or if something more sinister was at play, but the air felt charged with an energy she couldn't explain, like something ancient and forgotten was waking up inside the very bones of the mansion.

"What do you want from me?" she asked, her voice barely more than a whisper. The fear clawed at her chest, but there was something else too—something darker, something that made her question whether she was afraid of him, or afraid of the truth she had been running from.

The man stepped closer, his footsteps silent on the stone floor, as though he were gliding rather than walking. "It's not what I want, Ivy," he said, his voice a low, dangerous purr. "It's what you've already invited into your life. The truth is, you're already part of this world. Whether you understand it or not, whether you accept it or not, this is your fate."

Ivy's mind raced, her heart thudding painfully in her chest. This world he spoke of—this Court of Ashes—was it real? Was it all part of some twisted illusion? Or had she, somehow, crossed into a realm she wasn't supposed to touch?

Before she could speak, the mirror in the corner of the room caught her attention again. The reflection was still there, its twisted smile burned into her mind. It was a part of her now, wasn't it? The darkness in the glass wasn't some external force—it was a reflection of something she had buried inside herself for so long, something that had been clawing to get out.

"You see, Ivy," the man continued, his words sliding into her mind like poison, "you've always known there was more to you, more to this world than the mundane reality you've tried so desperately to hold onto. You've always felt it—the pull, the whispers in the dark corners of your mind, the hunger. You just didn't know what to call it. But now you do."

Ivy tried to step back, but her feet wouldn't move. The weight of his words, the weight of this place, held her in place, like chains that shackled her very soul. She wanted to scream, to run, but the air itself seemed to bind her, tightening around her chest with every passing second.

"What is this place?" Her voice cracked, raw with desperation. "What do you want from me? What do you want me to do?"

The man's lips curled into a smile that didn't reach his eyes, a smile that sent an icy chill down her spine. "This place is where everything ends, Ivy. It's where your path leads, whether you want it to or not. The Court of Ashes is the seat of power—the seat of truth. And you, my dear, you've come to claim your place."

A sudden gust of wind swept through the room, making the candles flicker and casting long, twisted shadows across the walls. Ivy's heart pounded as the air thickened, the temperature dropping so suddenly that her breath misted in the air. Her surroundings shifted again. The walls, the floors, the very space around her seemed to bend, and for a moment, she could swear she was standing on the edge of a vast, endless chasm—something beyond this world, beyond her comprehension.

And then, as if the room had opened into another realm entirely, she saw them.

Figures. Shapes—human, but not. Shadows, shifting forms, their faces obscured by masks of smoke and ash. They stood in a circle around her, silent and unmoving. Their presence filled the room, suffocating her, their eyes unseen but their power palpable. Ivy could feel them watching her, judging her. She wanted to scream, to run, but she stood frozen, unable to move.

"They are waiting for you, Ivy," the man said, his voice now an echo in the empty room, his form fading into the shadows. "They are the judges, the keepers of the Court. And now, you must decide—who are you, truly? Are you the girl who has been running all her life, or are you the one who will stand and face what's been hiding in the dark?"

Ivy's legs buckled beneath her, her knees hitting the cold stone floor. Her mind was spinning, her vision blurring as she gasped for air. She wanted to fight it. She wanted to scream, to tear herself away from this nightmare. But something in her—the part of her that had always been hungry for more, that had always sought the truth—pulled her forward. She was already here. And no matter how much she wished otherwise, she knew she would have to face whatever it was that waited in the Court of Ashes.

12

A Lover's Test

The air felt thick with anticipation, a pressure building in the silence that surrounded them. Ivy stood at the threshold of the Court of Ashes, the shadows swirling at her feet, twisting like sentient things. The man—his name still an enigma—stood across from her, his eyes unreadable, his posture tense with the weight of a challenge she could scarcely comprehend.

She hadn't asked for this. None of it. Her life had been simple once, a world of knowns and familiar faces. Now, nothing made sense. Every step forward felt like a descent into madness, and yet, she couldn't seem to stop herself from moving deeper into the labyrinth of this strange, cursed place.

"What is it you want from me?" Ivy asked again, her voice strained, her throat tight with the words that felt like nails scraping her insides. It was a question she had asked a hundred times, and each time, the answer had eluded her. But now, as she stared at him—at this man—something inside her began to shift, as though she were standing on the edge of something vast, something terrible and beautiful all at once.

The man did not answer immediately. Instead, he stepped closer, his steps slow, deliberate, as if the space between them were thickening with every passing moment. His eyes never left hers, and Ivy felt the weight of them, like invisible hands pulling at her, tugging her in every direction at once.

"You want answers, Ivy," he said, his voice soft but rich with meaning, as though he were savoring the words. "You want to understand this world you've found yourself in. But answers come with a price. And you..." He paused, letting the silence stretch between them like a taut wire, "You will have to prove yourself worthy of them."

Ivy frowned, her confusion deepening. She wanted to lash out, to demand that he stop playing games with her, stop toying with her mind, but there was something in his tone that made her hesitate. Prove yourself worthy? What did that even mean? Was there a test? A trial?

Her pulse quickened as he drew closer, the space between them narrowing with each step, and for the first time, she noticed the flicker of something strange in his eyes—something that wasn't just cold calculation or predatory intent. It was something softer, something that made her heart stutter, a glimmer of something—hope?—beneath the surface of his mask. But no, it couldn't be.

"You will face a choice, Ivy," he said, his voice dropping to a whisper, as if revealing a secret too dangerous to share aloud.

"A lover's test, if you will. You've been drawn here by more than mere curiosity. There is something else... something between us, isn't there?" His eyes darkened, and his gaze softened as though he had seen through the very fabric of her soul. "You can feel it, can't you? The pull, the thread that binds us."

Ivy took an instinctual step back, her body recoiling. But he was too close now. She could feel his presence like a heavy storm pressing in around her, suffocating her thoughts, drowning her senses. The attraction—the pull—he spoke of, was real, undeniable. But it terrified her. She had never felt anything like it before. Not for him. Not for anyone.

"I don't understand," Ivy whispered, her voice breaking with the weight of her confusion, her fear. "What are you asking me to do?"

He didn't respond at first. Instead, his gaze softened further, his eyes now tinged with something akin to sorrow, though it was fleeting—like the shadow of a dream that disappears upon waking. He reached out, his hand hovering just inches from hers, and in that moment, Ivy felt the intensity of his touch, the force of his presence. She could feel the heat radiating off him, the magnetic pull that drew her closer despite her every instinct to resist.

"You'll have to choose, Ivy," he said quietly. "Choose me, or choose yourself. But be warned: this test will reveal more than you ever wished to know. It will strip you bare, leave you exposed in ways you can't even imagine."

The words hung in the air between them, thick with meaning, weighted with consequences she wasn't ready to face. Her mind raced, her heart pounding in her chest, her body locked in place, unwilling to move even an inch closer to him. And yet, she couldn't help but feel it—feel the temptation, the allure of him, the possibility of something more.

A vision flashed in her mind—a flash of them together, tangled in a haze of passion, of fire and longing. It was intoxicating, a promise of something forbidden, something that beckoned to the deepest parts of her heart. But then, just as quickly, the vision shattered like glass, and the weight of reality crashed down on her.

This wasn't just about desire. This wasn't just about passion or love. It was something darker.

"Choose now, Ivy," he urged, his voice now barely a breath against her ear. "Choose before the moment passes."

But Ivy couldn't choose. Not yet. She was torn between the desire to fall into his arms, to give in to the dark beauty of this strange world, and the instinct to fight, to flee, to protect herself from whatever test awaited her.

And then, as if on cue, a whisper reached her ears—soft, insistent.

Run.

She didn't know if it was the man's voice or something else, something deeper, but the command was clear. The test had begun.

13

The Dance of Secrets

The music began before Ivy could even register where it was coming from. A soft, haunting melody, laced with the sound of strings that seemed to pull at her very soul. It echoed through the dark room, reverberating off the stone walls, carrying with it a sense of both longing and despair. Her breath caught in her throat as she turned, searching for the source, but there was nothing—nothing but the shadows that stretched like tendrils across the floor, reaching toward her, pulling her deeper into the heart of the Court of Ashes.

Her pulse quickened, the air thick with something unspoken, something ancient. The man—the one who had brought her here, the one who had promised her answers—was gone. She hadn't noticed him leave, hadn't even seen him move, but now the space between them felt immeasurable, as though the distance had grown into something insurmountable. A whisper of a movement caught her eye, and she turned, her heart racing.

In the far corner of the room, a door stood ajar, beckoning her with an eerie invitation. A sliver of light spilled from within, painting the darkness with pale, ghostly colors. The music, too, seemed to come from that direction, as if it were coming from the very heart of the mansion, from a place just beyond the door. There was something unnerving about it, something alluring. She couldn't explain it, but her feet seemed to move of their own accord, carried by an invisible pull.

As she walked toward the door, the floor beneath her feet creaked, the sound sharp and unsettling. The light from the crack in the door flickered like a dying flame, casting long shadows that twisted around her legs. She paused just before crossing the threshold, her hand hovering over the handle, but hesitation gripped her. Something about the door felt wrong— like stepping into a forbidden place, a place where secrets were kept, buried deep in the walls.

But there was no turning back. Not now. She had come too far.

The door opened with a groan, revealing a room bathed in the same haunting light. A large, polished mirror stood against the far wall, its surface smooth and reflective, though the edges were jagged and cracked, as though the glass had been shattered and pieced back together by invisible hands. And in front of the mirror stood the man—the one she had thought was gone, the one who had disappeared into the shadows.

But this time, he wasn't alone.

A woman stood beside him, her figure slender and ethereal,

draped in a gown of midnight blue that shimmered like the night sky. Her face was pale, her lips painted a dark crimson, and her hair flowed around her like a river of midnight. But it was her eyes—eyes that gleamed with an unsettling light—that caught Ivy's attention. They were cold, calculating, and though they were directed toward Ivy, there was no recognition in them. No warmth. Just an endless, soulless gaze.

The music stopped abruptly, and Ivy was left in the heavy silence, her breath caught in her throat. The woman's lips curled into a smile—cold, knowing—and she took a slow, deliberate step forward. The man beside her remained still, his posture rigid, as though he were part of the very walls.

"Well, well, Ivy," the woman said, her voice smooth, like velvet wrapped around a blade. "You've come far, haven't you? I wonder... How much do you really want to know?"

The words hung in the air like a challenge, an unspoken test. Ivy felt herself stiffen, a cold shiver running down her spine. She wanted to demand answers, to ask what was happening, what this place was, what they were doing here. But no words came. She could barely think. The weight of the situation pressed down on her, like a suffocating fog that stole her thoughts and made her feel small, insignificant.

The woman took another step forward, her eyes never leaving Ivy's face. "We know what you are, Ivy. We know what you've hidden from yourself for so long." She paused, as if savoring the moment, the fear that was rising within Ivy. "But the question is: Do you know who you really are?"

Ivy took a shaky step back, her mind racing. She had no idea what the woman meant. No idea how she could possibly know anything about her, about the secrets buried deep within her heart. And yet, somehow, it felt as though the woman did know. As though she could see into her very soul, could read every thought and fear Ivy had ever kept locked away.

The man—silent and unmoving beside her—finally spoke, his voice carrying a note of amusement. "She's right, Ivy. We all have our secrets. But some secrets..." He let the words trail off, a dark smile tugging at the corner of his lips. "Some secrets are more dangerous than others. And some, once uncovered, can never be put back."

The woman's eyes gleamed with something cold, something predatory. "You've danced with shadows long enough, Ivy. Now you must choose. You've come this far. But are you ready to dance with the truth?"

The question echoed in her mind, like a drumbeat. Dance with the truth. The words were not just an invitation—they were a summons. Ivy could feel it in her bones, the weight of her decision pressing down on her. To step forward was to acknowledge everything she had buried, everything she had feared. But to step back? To turn away? That would be to condemn herself to live in ignorance, in a never-ending cycle of half-truths and unspoken fears.

And in that moment, Ivy knew. The choice was never really hers to make. The dance of secrets was already in motion, and she was already a part of it.

14

A Cold Betrayal

The room was suffocating with silence, broken only by the soft, rhythmic thud of Ivy's heartbeat, pounding louder than the stillness that surrounded her. Her feet felt rooted to the floor, as if some unseen force had tethered her in place, forcing her to witness the scene unfolding before her. The woman stood there, a sinister smile playing on her lips as she looked at Ivy, her eyes gleaming with an unsettling malice. The man, too, remained motionless beside her, his face as unreadable as stone.

Ivy's mind raced, spinning with confusion and a sense of growing dread. She wanted to scream, to demand answers, to understand why everything felt so wrong. But the words lodged in her throat, choking her, leaving her silent as the tension in the air thickened.

The woman stepped closer, her movements fluid and calcu-lated, each step deliberate, each one bringing her closer to Ivy. The coldness in her gaze never faltered as she closed the distance between them. When she was within arm's reach, she stopped, tilting her head slightly, as if considering Ivy with an almost clinical detachment.

"Do you know what you've walked into, Ivy?" The woman's voice was a low, melodic hum, almost too sweet to be trusted. "Do you know the price of your curiosity? The cost of your desire for answers?"

Ivy opened her mouth to respond, but nothing came out. The words were there, tangled in her chest, but they wouldn't leave her. Her body felt heavy, as though it were fighting against her will, like something inside her was slowly eroding her strength, her resolve.

The woman laughed, a sound that was more like the cracking of ice than genuine amusement. "It's amusing, really," she continued, "how little you understand. How little you know about the game you've stepped into. But then again, you were never meant to understand. You were always a pawn in a much larger game."

A chill ran through Ivy, the kind of cold that sank deep into her bones and made her feel small, insignificant. She wanted to run, to escape from this place, but the air was thick with something that held her in place. It wasn't just fear. It was something far worse—something that twisted in her stomach like poison.

And then, as if to punctuate the horror of the moment, the man beside the woman spoke, his voice cutting through the air like a blade. "She's right, Ivy. You never stood a chance."

His words hit her like a slap, and she recoiled instinctively, her hands shaking at her sides. He—he—had been the one to pull her in, the one who had guided her to this point, the one who had promised her answers. And now, he was part of this? Part of whatever this woman was plotting?

"I trusted you," Ivy whispered, the words barely a breath, barely audible over the pounding of her heart in her ears.

The man didn't flinch. His expression remained impassive, cold, like the very walls that surrounded them. "Trust is a luxury you can't afford, Ivy," he said, his voice betraying no hint of emotion. "In this place, loyalty is fleeting. And betrayal? It's inevitable."

Ivy's stomach dropped, her mind reeling. This wasn't how it was supposed to be. She had come here looking for answers, for some semblance of truth, but now she realized—she had been nothing more than a pawn in their game, a piece on a board she didn't even understand.

The woman laughed again, and this time it was sharper, more malicious. She stepped toward Ivy, her eyes narrowing as she leaned in just close enough for Ivy to feel the cold of her breath on her skin.

"It's funny, really," the woman murmured, "how much you believed in him. How much you trusted him to protect you. He never cared for you, Ivy. He was never on your side. He was your test."

The words landed like stones, each one heavier than the last, sinking deep into her chest. She stumbled back, her mind reeling, her body fighting to stay upright. The man had—he had used her? Everything they had shared, everything she had trusted, had been a lie? Her heart, already cracked from the weight of their revelations, shattered completely. She felt the ground beneath her give way, and for a brief moment, everything around her seemed to spin, the walls closing in as the truth pressed against her like a vice.

The woman's hand shot out, grabbing Ivy by the wrist with a vice-like grip. "Don't look so surprised, Ivy. You were never meant to be his. You were never meant to win his favor, or his heart. You were always meant to be mine."

The words were like acid on her skin. They burned, they stung, and Ivy wanted to scream, but the woman's hold on her wrist was unyielding, crushing. The man watched them, his eyes cold, unfeeling, as though the pain Ivy felt was nothing more than an afterthought.

"You belong to me now," the woman continued, her voice dripping with venom. "Everything you thought you knew, everything you believed, has been shattered. And now, there is nothing left but me."

Ivy tried to pull away, but it was no use. The more she struggled, the tighter the woman's grip became, until Ivy felt her skin begin to bruise beneath the pressure. Her breaths came faster now, panic rising in her chest like a tide.

"No!" Ivy gasped, her voice breaking. "No, I—"

But the woman simply smiled, her eyes gleaming with cold satisfaction. "It's too late, Ivy. Your fate has already been sealed."

15

A Fire Within

The walls of the room seemed to close in around Ivy, the air thick with the weight of betrayal. She stood frozen, her mind scrambling to process the revelation, to comprehend the cruel twist of fate that had led her here. The man she had trusted—the one who had guided her through the labyrinth of shadows—was a part of the very thing she had feared the most. He had been lying to her from the beginning.

A cold fury began to stir deep within her chest, a fire that flickered at first, uncertain, like a flame caught in the wind. But the more she stood there, the more the words echoed in her ears, the more the truth settled into her bones. The fire grew, its heat spreading through her veins, igniting something inside her that had long been dormant. She felt the heat in her fingertips, in the pit of her stomach, in the very marrow of her bones. A strength she hadn't known existed was slowly building inside her, pushing back the suffocating cold that had surrounded her.

She could feel their eyes on her—the man and the woman, both watching her with something akin to amusement. The woman's smile was sharp, predatory, and the man's expression remained unreadable, his eyes cold and calculating. Ivy clenched her fists at her sides, her nails biting into her palms as the fire inside her flared, stronger now, hotter, like the beginning of a storm.

"I should have known," Ivy said, her voice barely above a whisper at first, but as the fire grew, so did the strength of her words. "I should have known you were never what you seemed."

The woman's laugh was like ice breaking. "You were never meant to understand, Ivy. You're a pawn. A vessel. You've always been part of the game." Her voice dropped lower, laced with a deadly finality. "And now, you're mine."

The words struck Ivy like a blow to the chest, but instead of crumbling, instead of giving in to the weight of them, she felt the fire inside her burn brighter. She wasn't their pawn. She wasn't anyone's to control. They thought they could use her, manipulate her, but they didn't understand her, not really.

The man took a step forward, his eyes narrowing as he studied her, sensing the shift in her energy. "You're angry, Ivy," he said, his voice softer now, almost like a warning. "And that's dangerous. You don't know what you're dealing with."

Ivy's chest rose and fell with every breath, her body trembling not with fear, but with the heat of her rising fury. "You don't get to control me," she spat, her voice thick with defiance. "Not anymore."

The flames inside her were no longer just an internal force—they were real, physical, tangible. She could feel the heat building, the energy swirling around her like a storm waiting to break. It was as though her very being had become the furnace, the source of an inferno that could not be extinguished.

In a single, fluid motion, she thrust her hand toward the mirror across the room. The reflection that had once mocked her now trembled, the glass vibrating in response to the intensity of the power that surged through her. The woman stepped back, her eyes widening in disbelief as the air itself seemed to warp around Ivy, the very temperature of the room rising to an unbearable heat.

"You think you can fight this?" the woman sneered. "You think you can fight me?"

But Ivy wasn't listening. Her focus was on the fire within her, the energy that was now coursing through her with unstoppable force. The mirror cracked, its surface fracturing as the flames grew stronger, as if the very fabric of reality was bending under the weight of her will.

The man watched her, his face betraying a flicker of something—a hint of recognition, perhaps—before it was quickly masked by his usual, unreadable expression. He took another step forward, but this time, there was no malice in his movement. It was almost as if he were testing her, waiting to see just how far she would go.

"Don't," he said, his voice low, almost pleading. But there was no authority in his tone, no control. The power Ivy had unleashed was something he couldn't stop. He hadn't anticipated this, hadn't expected her to awaken the fire within her so completely.

"I don't need your permission," Ivy responded, her words clear, cutting through the thick air like a blade. Her hand moved again, this time toward the woman who had stood beside the man, the one who had reveled in her confusion and fear. The woman flinched, her eyes flashing with fury as the flames swirled around Ivy, growing stronger with every second.

"Enough!" the woman hissed, but Ivy could hear the tremor in her voice, the uncertainty.

The fire surged one final time, a burst of heat so intense that the room seemed to implode in on itself. The air around her shimmered, the flames now a blazing force that radiated from her skin. For a moment, Ivy felt weightless, as though she were standing on the edge of the world, her body filled with a power that was ancient and untouchable.

Then, as the flames flickered out, the room fell silent. The fire within Ivy simmered, but it was still there, a part of her, a force that could never be extinguished. She stood in the middle of the room, breathing heavily, her body trembling with the aftershock of what she had unleashed.

The woman and the man stood frozen, their eyes fixed on her, and for the first time, Ivy saw something in their eyes—a flicker of fear. And in that moment, she realized that they were no longer the ones in control. She was.

16

The Hidden Room

The flames had burned out, leaving nothing but the faint smell of smoke in the air and a trail of cracked glass scattered across the floor. Ivy's breath was ragged, her heart still pounding from the surge of energy that had almost consumed her. She had never felt anything like it before—the way her body had ignited, the way her power had surged like a wave, uncontainable, unstoppable. But now, the room was eerily still. The mirrors, once shattered and fractured under the weight of her anger, had settled into a glassy silence, reflecting her disheveled figure with a strange detachment.

The man and the woman were no longer standing where they had been. It was as if they had never been there at all, swallowed up by the shadows that had grown deeper, darker in the wake of the storm she had unleashed.

Ivy stepped cautiously forward, her feet heavy with uncertainty, every step a reminder of the moment that had changed everything. Her mind was spinning, still processing the anger, the betrayal, the rush of power. She didn't know what was happening to her, didn't know how to control what she had just felt. But there was no time for questions now. There was only the pressing need to find out what lay beyond this broken world.

She looked around the room, her eyes flicking from one shadowed corner to the next, searching for something—anything—that could explain the twisted game they had been playing with her. But the room offered no answers. The door that had once led her into this forsaken place remained shut, its frame solid and unmoving, as if it had never been opened at all. The mirror, now fragmented, held no reflection of her but instead seemed to gaze back at her with an ominous emptiness.

Then, a soft click echoed through the room.

It was barely perceptible at first, but Ivy froze, her senses sharp. She felt it before she heard it—the subtle shift in the air, the subtle movement in the floorboards beneath her. Her heart skipped a beat as she turned toward the source of the sound. A wall near the far corner of the room, previously imperceptible in its stillness, now seemed to pulse with a strange, barely discernible energy.

She took a step toward it, her pulse quickening.

The wall was unremarkable at first glance, nothing but stone, old and cracked in places, like the rest of the mansion. But there was something different about it now—a faint glow emanated from the cracks, as though the very walls were alive, breathing.

Slowly, she reached out, her fingers brushing against the surface of the stone. It was warm to the touch, a stark contrast to the coldness of the rest of the room. Her fingers slid over the smooth surface, tracing the jagged edges of the cracks, until she found it—the faint outline of a hidden door.

A shiver ran down Ivy's spine as she pressed her palm against the stone. The glow intensified beneath her hand, and then, with a soft rumble, the door creaked open, revealing a passage beyond. The air that poured out from the darkness beyond was thick, like the air before a storm, charged with an unspoken promise of things yet to come.

Without thinking, Ivy stepped through the doorway.

The passage was narrow, the walls close enough that she had to hold her breath as she squeezed through. The air was musty and thick with dust, but there was something else, something heavier, clinging to the darkness like a presence that was neither alive nor dead. Her footfalls echoed in the narrow space, the sound unnervingly loud against the silence that enveloped her. The passage twisted and turned, winding deeper into the heart of the mansion, and Ivy's senses were on high alert, her every instinct screaming at her to turn back.

But she couldn't.

She had come this far, and there was no turning back now.

The passage finally opened up into a cavernous room, its size impossible to judge in the dim light. At first, she thought the room was empty, but then her eyes adjusted to the darkness, and she saw them—objects, relics, scattered across the floor like offerings to some long-forgotten god. The air was thick with the scent of old wood and decay, and there was a strange, metallic tang that seemed to hang in the air, as though the room itself was a place of memories better left undisturbed.

At the far end of the room, something glimmered in the darkness. Ivy's breath hitched as she stepped closer, her heart thundering in her chest. It was a chest, old and weathered, covered in dust and cobwebs, but the lock glowed faintly, as though it were alive. Her fingers trembled as she reached for it, the warmth from the hidden door still lingering on her skin.

The moment her fingers touched the lock, the room shifted. The walls groaned and the floor beneath her feet seemed to tremble, as though the very structure of the mansion had awakened. The chest creaked open slowly, revealing a dark void within. Ivy's breath caught in her throat as the darkness seemed to swirl and pull at her, as though something was reaching out from within, beckoning her closer.

A voice, low and guttural, whispered from the darkness. "You've found it."

Ivy froze, the air around her thick with dread. The voice was familiar, but it didn't belong here. It didn't belong to anything she knew.

"Come closer," the voice coaxed, and Ivy's legs moved of their own accord, drawn forward by an unseen force. The chest continued to glow, its darkness deepening as she approached, its presence suffocating, irresistible.

"Come closer, Ivy," the voice repeated, now just a breath away from her ear. "It's time to face what you've been running from."

And in that moment, Ivy understood. The room was not empty. It had never been empty. It had been waiting for her.

17

Falling Through the Flames

The passage opened up into a vast, cavernous space, its size impossible to fathom from the narrow corridor she had just emerged from. The air in the room was thick and oppressive, heavier than it had been anywhere else in the mansion. There was a faint crackle in the air, a low hum that vibrated through Ivy's bones, making the hairs on her arms stand up. Her breath came in shallow gasps, her chest tight as she took in the darkened room before her.

At first, she couldn't see the walls, only the vast, smoky expanse stretching before her. The light was dim, the shadows stretching and writhing as if alive. But then her eyes began to adjust, and she saw it. The floor was a patchwork of scorched stone, blackened and cracked, as if something had burned through it. Trails of red-hot embers smoldered in the gaps, flickering like dying stars. The temperature was unbearable, searing, but it wasn't the heat that made Ivy's heart race; it was the overwhelming feeling of being watched.

There was something in this room, something old and ancient, its presence suffocating, pressing in from all sides. It felt like being at the center of a storm, the wind howling around her, the fire threatening to consume her from every angle. She instinctively stepped forward, her boots clicking softly against the stone as she moved, though each step felt like a betrayal, a challenge to something unseen and powerful.

Her mind reeled, her thoughts spinning faster than she could grasp them. What was this place? Why had it been hidden from her? More importantly, who had brought her here—and why?

The room seemed to stretch endlessly, the shadows bending and curling like darkened tendrils, drawing her further into the unknown. She swallowed hard, pushing down the nausea rising in her throat, but still, she couldn't shake the feeling that something was moving in the darkness.

A sudden noise broke the silence—a scrape, followed by a low growl. Ivy froze, her heart hammering in her chest, her pulse a steady thrum of panic in her ears. Her breath caught in her throat as she scanned the room, her eyes darting between the shifting shadows. There, in the distance, a figure stepped forward. Its form was indistinct, wrapped in shadows that seemed to twist around it like a cloak. The creature—or whatever it was—moved with a fluidity that was almost too smooth, too unnatural.

Ivy's instinct was to retreat, but she didn't. She couldn't. There was no way out, no path but forward. She had to know, had to understand what this place was. But still, she hesitated, her every muscle trembling in anticipation.

"Who's there?" she called out, her voice shaking, betraying her uncertainty. She cursed herself the moment the words left her lips. There was no hiding the fear in her tone. She was alone here, surrounded by the unknown.

The figure didn't answer, but it moved closer. Ivy's breath hitched as the shadows around the figure seemed to pulse and ripple, like the flames of an eternal fire, ready to devour her whole. It was close now, so close that Ivy could see the glint of its eyes—two cold, unblinking orbs of molten gold that locked onto her with a malevolent hunger.

And then, without warning, the flames erupted.

It was like falling through the fire itself. The world seemed to tilt as the floor beneath her gave way, the ground crumbling, breaking apart like brittle glass. Ivy screamed, her voice drowned by the roar of the fire that exploded from the cracks. The heat enveloped her, scorching her skin, her hair catching the inferno that rose from below. Her body was wrenched from the ground, sent spiraling into the air as the flames seemed to reach for her, clawing at her, tugging at her very soul.

She felt herself falling, falling through the flames, her body weightless in the chaos. Her heart pounded in her chest, her head spinning, and for a moment, she couldn't tell if she was soaring or plummeting. The smoke burned in her lungs, the heat blinding, suffocating. She thought she could hear whispers—soft, insistent, murmurs in a language she couldn't understand—but they were lost in the roaring tempest around her.

Her body twisted, spiraling down into the abyss, the flames licking at her skin as though they wanted to consume her whole. She reached out, instinctively, for anything to grab onto, but there was nothing—only endless darkness and the unrelenting heat of the fire.

And then, just as suddenly as it had begun, it stopped.

The air shifted, the weight of the flames pulling back like a retreating tide. Ivy gasped for breath, her chest heaving as the world snapped back into focus. She was lying on cold stone, her limbs heavy, her body trembling with the aftershock of the fall.

But she was no longer in the same place. The room—if it could even be called a room—was different. It was smaller, confined, the walls constricting around her. The faint glow of firelight flickered in the distance, casting long, twisted shadows on the floor.

Her hand brushed against the cold stone, and she realized with a jolt that she was not alone. She wasn't sure when they had arrived, but they were here—standing just beyond the shadows, watching her. Eyes. Eyes filled with endless secrets, staring back at her, patient and eternal.

And in that moment, Ivy understood. This wasn't just a test. This wasn't just a game. She had fallen through the flames, through the very heart of this cursed place—and now, there was no turning back.

18

The Heart of the Storm

Ivy's body hit the ground with a sickening thud, the shock of impact rattling through her bones. For a moment, everything was nothing but darkness, her senses overwhelmed by the disorienting spin of the fall and the suffocating heat that clung to the air like a living thing. Her pulse pounded in her ears, the thrum of it mingling with the crackling of the flames that still licked at the edges of her consciousness. Her eyes snapped open, and she gasped for air, her lungs burning, as though the very air had been poisoned by the firestorm that raged around her.

But it wasn't just the flames.

The room was alive.

The walls around her were shifting—shifting as if the very fabric of the world itself was tearing apart. She could hear the low, ominous growl of the storm, a dark rumble that seemed to come from deep within the earth, vibrating through her bones.

She pushed herself to her knees, her hands trembling as she wiped the sweat and ash from her forehead. Her legs felt weak, her body heavy, but the fire—the fire—still burned in her veins. That fire, that power, was her only anchor in the chaos of this place.

She had to move.

Slowly, painfully, Ivy pushed herself up from the scorched earth. Her vision swam, the world tilting as the ground shifted beneath her. The heat of the flames was now a distant memory, replaced by an overwhelming pressure that seemed to crush the air itself. The storm—no, the force—surrounding her was like a pulse, a heartbeat too strong, too loud. It was everywhere, in the air, in the ground, in the very space between her breath.

But somewhere, deep in the heart of this chaos, she could feel something pulling her. A sense of purpose. A need to go forward, to find whatever was at the center of this storm, whatever waited for her in the eye of the destruction.

Ivy stumbled forward, her legs unsteady beneath her, each step a battle against the wind that howled around her. The air itself seemed to burn, sharp like needles, slicing at her skin, but it wasn't the physical pain that made her falter—it was the presence. It was like being surrounded by a thousand eyes, a thousand minds, all watching her, all waiting.

And then, through the madness, she saw it.

A figure standing at the center of the room, shrouded in a

cloak of shifting shadows. Its outline was distorted, constantly changing, like a mirage flickering in the heart of a desert. But Ivy could feel its gaze. Could feel the weight of its attention pressing down on her.

She didn't know how she knew, but she did. This was it. This was the source of the storm. The heart of the darkness.

The figure lifted its head, and Ivy's breath caught in her throat. Its eyes—pale, unblinking, empty—locked onto hers. The figure took a step toward her, and with that movement, the storm grew louder, the winds howling as though in response to its will. Ivy felt herself being pushed backward, her body swaying with the intensity of the air around her. It was like standing at the edge of a cliff, with nothing but darkness below.

But she couldn't stop now. She couldn't turn away.

"Why?" she croaked, her voice barely audible over the roar of the storm. "Why is this happening?"

The figure didn't answer. Instead, it raised one hand, fingers elongated and pale, the shadow of its hand stretching unnaturally long as it reached toward her. Ivy's heart stopped, her instincts screaming at her to run, to escape, but her feet were rooted to the ground.

The hand touched her chest, and the world cracked.

A sudden jolt of energy shot through Ivy, a violent, searing wave of power that rushed through her body like a lightning strike. Her breath was stolen from her as her entire being was overwhelmed with the sheer force of the connection. For a split second, it felt like her soul was being torn apart—like she was being pulled in a thousand directions at once. But through the chaos, through the storm that raged both inside and outside her, Ivy saw it.

A vision.

The truth.

The figure in front of her wasn't just a being of shadow. It was her. Or rather, it was the other half of her—an echo, a reflection, a dark counterpart forged from the very fire that had awakened within her. She had been brought here to this moment, to this storm, because of what she was. Because of the power that was hers by birthright, a power that had been dormant for so long, waiting for the right time to awaken.

And now, that time had come.

The storm was her. It was her rage, her fury, her fear, all compressed into this single, terrible moment. The flames had been just the beginning. This—this was the true test. To face herself. To face the power that could either destroy her or set her free.

The figure's eyes never left hers, its expression unreadable, as if it were waiting for her to understand, for her to make the choice. But there was no time left. The storm was building again, growing stronger, the winds howling louder, the shadows closing in.

You must decide, the voice whispered in her mind, a voice that was both her own and not her own. Will you fall through the flames again? Or will you rise?

With that, Ivy stepped forward into the heart of the storm.

19

A Forbidden Alliance

The room pulsed with an unbearable tension, the air thick with the oppressive weight of impending doom. Ivy stood motionless, her chest heaving as she tried to grasp what was happening. The figure before her—this thing, this presence that seemed to defy all logic—had touched her, its icy hand sending a shockwave of power through her. It was like the touch of death itself, cold and unyielding, and yet there was something else—something familiar, something she couldn't place.

The winds that had howled around her now began to die down, their ferocity waning, but the storm still hung in the air like a specter, its presence not fully gone. The figure before her was still, its head tilted slightly as it studied her, its eyes as empty and hollow as the vast, burning chasm she had fallen into.

"You shouldn't be here," the voice came at last, deep and resonant, like the rumble of thunder far off in the distance. It was not a voice that belonged to a living thing. It was ancient, guttural, yet somehow familiar—familiar in a way that made Ivy's heart race.

"I never asked to be here," Ivy replied, her voice trembling with a mixture of fear and defiance. Her legs felt weak beneath her, but the fire that had burned within her still simmered, a steady reminder that she was not as powerless as she felt.

The figure didn't flinch at her words. "No," it said, its voice like the scrape of stone against stone, "but you have come nonetheless. And now, there is no turning back."

Ivy swallowed hard, the words sinking deep into her chest. No turning back. She had known that from the moment she had stepped into this madness, from the moment she had felt the darkness close in around her, but hearing it spoken aloud, from this thing—this entity that seemed older than time itself— made the truth of it all the more suffocating.

"I don't understand," Ivy said, taking a step forward, her voice laced with frustration. "What do you want from me? What is this place?"

The figure's eyes never wavered from hers. "This place?" it echoed. "This is not a place. It is a force. A convergence of powers beyond your comprehension. Powers that have waited eons for someone... like you."

"Like me?" Ivy's voice cracked. "I'm just a—"

"Just a pawn?" The figure's lips twitched, the barest hint of a smile curling at the corners of its mouth. "Yes. You are that, and more. But you are not here by accident. You were chosen. Chosen to tip the scales."

"Chosen for what?" Ivy demanded, her voice rising with a mixture of anger and fear. "What do you want me to do?"

The figure stepped forward, its movement smooth and unnerving, like a shadow slipping through the fabric of reality itself. "I want you to understand that you are not the only player in this game. You are a piece, but there are others. And those others... have been moving against you. Moving against me."

Ivy's mind raced. "The man I trusted," she murmured, her thoughts crashing together in a flood of realization. "He... he was part of this?"

"Yes," the figure said, its voice darkening with disdain. "A pawn, just like you. A tool to be used and discarded."

Ivy took another step back, the weight of the truth pressing down on her. "And you? Who are you really?"

The figure's smile deepened, its form shifting in the flickering light of the embers that still clung to the shadows. "I am not what you think. Not what you've been led to believe." The shadows around it seemed to swirl as if they had a life of their own. "But I can help you. I can give you what you seek."

A cold shiver ran down Ivy's spine. "What's the catch?"

"A forbidden alliance," the figure replied, its voice thick with a power that seemed to seep from the walls around them. "You want to stop them. The ones who have deceived you. The ones who have controlled you. I can give you the power to break their hold. But it will cost you."

The words hung in the air like a poisonous fog, thick and suffocating. Ivy's breath caught, her body tensing as the weight of the offer pressed upon her. She could feel the pull—the lure of the power it offered, the chance to strike back at the people who had lied to her, used her, torn her apart.

"I'll do anything," she said before she could stop herself, her voice a harsh whisper, raw with desperation.

The figure tilted its head, the faintest glint of amusement flashing in its empty eyes. "Anything? How convenient." It stepped closer, the temperature around them plummeting, the air becoming thick with the taste of something darker, something far more dangerous.

"What do I have to do?" Ivy asked, her voice steady now, the fire inside her sparking once more. She had no choice. If this was the only way to escape this nightmare, to find the truth and take control of her fate, then she would follow it. Even if it meant forging an alliance with something she didn't understand.

"Swear yourself to me," the figure intoned, its voice like a chant. "Give me your loyalty, and in return, I will give you the strength to burn down your enemies. To rise above them all."

Ivy hesitated. The weight of the decision was enormous, pressing down on her chest, filling her with a cold foreboding. But she had come too far to turn back now. She had already fallen through the fire, and she wasn't going to let it consume her.

"I swear," she said, the words escaping her lips before she could second-guess herself.

The figure smiled, a cold, unfeeling smile that made Ivy's skin crawl. "Then it is done."

20

The Unseen Hand

The air around Ivy seemed to thicken, as if the very atmosphere had become a dense, impenetrable fog, swirling with something far older and far more dangerous than she had ever imagined. The figure that stood before her, its form still obscured by shadows, seemed to pulse with power, with an energy so potent it made the ground beneath her tremble. The weight of its gaze pressed down on her, suffocating, unyielding. Every instinct screamed at her to flee, to run from the unknown, but her feet were rooted to the floor, unwilling to obey the commands of her terrified mind.

She knew something was coming.

Something far worse than anything she had already faced.

"You think you understand, don't you?" The figure's voice sliced through the air, the words dripping with a mocking tone, but there was something else there—something darker, a menace lurking just beneath the surface. "You think you're in control. That you can fight this. But there is a power far older than you. Far older than even I. And it is already here."

The last word hung in the air like a thread, pulling at the edges of Ivy's resolve. She forced herself to stand taller, to meet the figure's unseen eyes with all the defiance she could muster.

"I don't need to understand," Ivy shot back, her voice shaking but steadying with every word. "All I need to know is that I'm not going down without a fight."

The figure chuckled—low, rumbling, like the sound of distant thunder. "Ah," it mused, "the fire of defiance. How predictable. But you are wrong, Ivy. It is not your strength that will decide the outcome of this game. It never has been."

A cold gust of wind swept through the room, and the temperature dropped sharply. Ivy's breath formed visible clouds in the suddenly frigid air. She wrapped her arms around herself, not out of cold, but to hold herself together. It was as if the world itself was folding in on her, each breath she took drawing her deeper into a vortex she couldn't escape.

"And just what is it you think will decide?" she asked, her voice small but her gaze unwavering.

The figure didn't respond immediately. Instead, the shadows around it seemed to ripple, swirling in patterns too complex for her to follow, as if some invisible hand was weaving them together, pulling them into a tapestry that threatened to swallow her whole. The ground beneath her feet began to shift, the stone under her feet groaning as if alive, as if it too were part of the intricate web she was becoming entangled in.

"I am no fool," Ivy said, more to herself than to the figure, though her words echoed in the chamber. "I know you're not what you appear to be. You think you've tricked me, but you haven't."

A strange silence hung between them, thick and suffocating, until the figure's voice broke it once again. "You think you're fighting the right enemy? You think your struggles are your own? You are nothing—just a piece in a game you do not understand."

Ivy flinched, her chest tightening, but she held her ground. "You're wrong. I am not a pawn. I will never be a pawn again."

The figure's laughter was low, echoing, a dark, hollow sound that seemed to seep into the very bones of the mansion. "We all are," it said, its voice now turning darker, more sinister. "You think you've uncovered all the secrets. That you've seen all the cards. But the hand that plays this game is not one you can see, Ivy. It is already in motion, and it has already claimed its winners. And you? You're just a piece of the sacrifice. A mere distraction."

Something deep within Ivy stirred, something cold, something hard. She felt it, rising in her chest—a fire, yes, but not the same one that had burned before. This fire was not born of anger or defiance. It was born of a knowledge she had avoided, a truth she had buried deep within herself. She could feel it now, beneath the surface of her skin, pressing against her, as though the very blood in her veins were calling out to the unseen force that had guided her all along.

The ground beneath her shifted again.

This time, there was no denying it.

She was no longer in control.

A sudden pressure constricted around her, pulling her toward the figure, her body unwilling to fight the invisible force that had wrapped itself around her like chains. The storm that had begun to form in the distance now roared to life. Dark clouds swirled above her, gathering in an impenetrable vortex, swirling with the kind of destructive energy that made her bones ache, made her soul tremble with a fear she couldn't contain.

"You want control, Ivy?" The figure's voice was a rasp now, like nails scraping against a chalkboard. "Then come. Come to the heart of the storm, where your power will either break you or set you free. Come and claim your place. But be warned, you will not leave here the same."

Ivy opened her mouth to speak, but no words came out. Instead, she felt a force—a hand, an unseen hand—reach into her very soul, grabbing hold of her deepest fears and desires. It twisted, pulling her further into the storm, deeper into the heart of it.

Her body resisted, her heart screamed, but it was too late.

The storm had her now. And there was no escaping the price that would come with it.

III

Part Three

Embers of Redemption

21

The Betrayer's Mask

Ivy felt the ground shift beneath her feet once again, this time with more force, as if the very foundation of the room were about to crumble. Her breath caught in her throat, a sharp instinct warning her of the danger that loomed just beyond her reach. The figure before her—this being of shadows and whispered threats—seemed to grow in stature, its presence swallowing the space around her, its power a living, breathing thing that twisted the very air.

The dark laughter still echoed in her ears, curling around her mind like smoke, choking her thoughts, blurring her focus. The words it spoke clung to her, each one a weight she couldn't shake. "You are a distraction," it had said. "A pawn in a game you do not understand." Ivy's chest tightened at the implication. It felt like an iron vice squeezing the breath from her lungs. How much of this was true? Was she really just a player in a game too vast for her to comprehend?

"You think you know who the enemy is," the figure continued, its voice a low, rasping whisper now, as though the very walls of the room conspired to carry its words directly to her soul. "But there is one closer than you realize, Ivy. One who wears a mask of trust, a mask of friendship."

Ivy's heart stuttered, the name rising unbidden in her mind. "No..." she whispered, the word barely leaving her lips.

The figure seemed to sense her fear, its invisible gaze locking onto her with a knowing hunger. "Yes," it said, its tone sharpening, like the crack of a whip. "He has been beside you all this time, watching, listening, manipulating. The one who promised you salvation. The one who claimed to be your ally."

Ivy's pulse quickened as the figure's words sank in, each syllable twisting in her chest. Her mind reeled. Her thoughts scrambled for purchase, for something to hold onto, but they slipped like sand through her fingers. Her vision blurred, and for a moment, the room around her seemed to shift, the shadows pulling together like a canvas painting, revealing the shape of a man standing just out of reach—his face half-hidden by a mask.

No.

The thought crashed into her with the force of a tidal wave. She couldn't breathe, couldn't think, as the weight of the realization hit her like a sledgehammer. It was him.

The person she had trusted more than anyone. The one who had helped her through the darkest moments of this twisted journey. The one who had made her believe that, despite everything, there was still hope.

All of it, a lie.

All of it.

The ground trembled again, and Ivy took a stumbling step back, her heart racing in her chest, her mind trying to piece together the fractured images of her memories. She thought of him—his soft words, his comforting presence, his smile that always seemed to promise her safety. She thought of how he had been there when everything felt like it was falling apart, how he had convinced her that together they could escape the storm, that they could fight the darkness.

But the figure before her... it was right. He had been there. Watching. Waiting. Manipulating.

"You knew," Ivy whispered, her voice hoarse, barely a sound. "You knew all along."

"Yes," the figure said softly, a trace of satisfaction in its voice. "You've always been blind, Ivy. But the mask is slipping now, and when you finally see the truth, it will burn you."

Ivy's knees nearly gave out beneath her as the words hit her, one after the other, each a hammer to her already broken soul. She staggered backward, her mind refusing to accept what was happening. The figure's laughter swirled around her, maddening, echoing in the cavernous room.

"How could he?" Ivy choked out, her voice trembling with a mixture of heartbreak and fury. "How could he betray me? After everything we've been through?"

The figure tilted its head, its form still indistinct, its presence pressing down on her like a dark cloud. "It was never about you, Ivy. It was never about your cause. It was always about power. And he, just like you, was a tool. A means to an end."

Ivy's hands clenched into fists, her nails digging into her palms. The air around her crackled, thick with the charged tension that swirled like a storm cloud, but beneath the fury, beneath the pain, something else began to burn—a deep, cold rage, one that was sharper than anything she had ever known.

She had been played.

All of it had been part of a game—a game she had never understood, one where she had been nothing more than a pawn. And the man she had trusted? He was no different. His face had been a mask, his words a deception, and now, the truth lay bare before her like a broken mirror, reflecting nothing but the fractured pieces of her own shattered heart.

"You're wrong," Ivy said, her voice low, dangerous. "I'm not a pawn. I'll never be a pawn again."

The figure seemed to smile, though its face was hidden in shadow. "We'll see."

Ivy's chest tightened with a new resolve, a burning desire to see this through, to face whatever storm lay ahead. She would not let the darkness consume her. She would find him, the betrayer, the one who had lied to her so thoroughly. And when she found him, there would be no forgiveness. Only justice.

The figure before her dissolved into the shadows, its presence receding like smoke in the wind, leaving Ivy alone in the center of the room. But her thoughts were no longer consumed by the figure's words. No, now they were consumed by one thing— one question.

Where was he?

22

Burning Bridges

The moment the door slammed shut behind her, Ivy felt the weight of the world collapse inward. She stood in the hallway, her back pressed against the cold stone wall, her chest rising and falling with ragged breaths. The flickering torches lining the corridor threw dancing shadows on the walls, but all she could see was his face—his face. The face she had once trusted. The face that had once promised her safety, now twisted by betrayal.

How long had he been lying to her? How long had he been playing his part, pretending to be her ally, her confidant, when all along, he was the architect of the very destruction that had consumed her life?

A sharp, guttural sound tore from Ivy's throat as she slid down the wall, her knees buckling beneath her. The coldness of the stone floor seeped into her skin, but she barely noticed. The pain that throbbed through her chest was far more intense, a kind of grief and rage that swallowed everything in its wake.

She had trusted him. She had believed in him.

How could I have been so blind?

Her mind raced, replaying every moment, every conversation, every shared glance. She thought of the first time they had met, the way he had offered his hand, how genuine he had seemed. How convincing. The moments they shared, the quiet talks late at night, where he had listened to her, comforted her when the shadows closed in. How could it all have been a lie?

And then the last encounter, the moment she had confronted him, demanded the truth. She had seen the flicker in his eyes, the hesitation. Had he planned for that too? Had he known she would finally break and demand the answers? She could still hear his words echoing in her mind, the coldness in his voice when he finally confessed. The way he had stood there, unshaken, as if everything he had done was justified. As if he had done it all for her.

She was shaking now, trembling from head to toe as the reality of the situation hit her like a physical blow. She had never truly known him. He had never been who he said he was. She had been nothing but a pawn in his game, a means to an end. All those promises, all those whispered assurances in the dead of night—it had all been nothing more than smoke and mirrors.

Ivy's hand clenched into a fist, her nails digging into the flesh of her palm as she forced herself to stand. She couldn't let this break her. She wouldn't let it break her. But the rage was boiling inside her, a storm that threatened to explode. She wanted to scream, wanted to tear down everything in her path, to make him pay for the way he had twisted her life into this nightmare.

But as the anger surged through her, something else began to take hold. Something darker. Something that whispered at the edges of her mind, urging her toward a choice she knew would change everything.

She had been betrayed. But she was still standing. And she was stronger than this.

With a sudden clarity, Ivy pushed herself off the wall and stood upright, her face flushed with determination. There was no going back. She had crossed the point of no return when she had walked into that room, when she had confronted him. The bridge between them had already been burned.

The truth was out. And there was no place for him in her life anymore.

Her eyes narrowed. She was done running, done playing games. He thought he had won, that his manipulation had cornered her, but he was wrong. She would destroy everything he had built, piece by piece, until nothing was left but the ruins of his lies.

Ivy turned and walked toward the staircase, each step a deliberate motion, her heart pounding as she ascended. She had to find him. She had to make him face the consequences of what he had done. This time, the roles were reversed. This time, she was the one in control.

As she reached the top of the staircase, she stopped for a moment, her gaze lingering on the door that led to the inner sanctum of the mansion. The place where he had hidden himself all these months. Where his lies had taken root and grown. Where everything had gone wrong. She could still hear his voice in her head, his parting words as she had walked away from him, leaving him to stew in his own guilt.

"I never wanted this for you," he had said, his voice breaking with a hint of desperation. "You have to understand, Ivy. I did it because I had no choice."

But now, standing in the cold, dim light of the hallway, Ivy realized something. She wasn't the one who needed to understand. She wasn't the one who had failed. He was the one who had crossed the line. He was the one who had made his choices. And now he would pay.

With a deep breath, Ivy's hand reached for the door handle. It felt cold beneath her touch, like the very metal was in league with the storm that raged inside her. She hesitated for just a moment, then turned the handle, the creak of the door breaking the stillness like the crack of thunder.

She stepped inside.

The shadows that filled the room seemed to push against her, as though they were alive, waiting for her to make her move. The dim light from the single candle on the table flickered weakly, casting long, shifting shadows on the walls. But Ivy wasn't afraid of the dark anymore. She had learned to live with it, had learned to wield it, to make it her ally.

And now, she would burn the bridges that had led her here—one way or another.

23

In the Ashes of Hope

The air in the chamber was thick with the smell of smoke. It was faint at first, a distant whisper of burning wood, but as Ivy stepped into the room, the scent grew stronger, more pungent, until it choked her lungs with its bitterness. The stone walls were marked with black streaks, scorched by fire long forgotten, the charred remains of something that had once been whole. The flickering light from the torches cast long shadows across the floor, bending and twisting, as if the darkness itself were alive.

Ivy stood motionless, her breath shallow, her heart hammering against her ribs. She had expected this moment. No—she had known it would come, but knowing something in your mind and facing it head-on were two very different things. Her body trembled, and her hands shook as she gripped the stone ledge before her, her knuckles white.

Before her lay the remnants of everything she had fought for. The fragments of the hope she had once believed in. The hope that had sustained her through the darkest moments, the hope that had kept her pushing forward even when every step felt like walking through fire.

Was it all a lie?

The question circled in her mind like a vulture, but it was not the question she could allow herself to answer—not yet. There were too many unknowns, too many pieces of this twisted puzzle still scattered, half-hidden in the ashes. But one thing was certain: She had been betrayed, and she could never return to the life she had once known.

The figure had revealed it all to her—him. The one she had trusted. The one she had allowed into her life, into her heart. The one who had always promised her safety, protection, and understanding. But now she knew. Now she understood. The mask he had worn had slipped, and behind it was nothing but cold calculation, a hunger for power, for control. Everything, every moment of connection between them, had been a carefully constructed façade.

He was never my ally.

The thought hit her with a wave of nausea, and she swayed on her feet, almost falling. Her vision blurred, and for a moment, she wasn't sure where she was. The room seemed to pulse, the walls closing in around her. She pressed a hand to her forehead, trying to steady herself, but the pain of the betrayal was a gnawing ache deep in her chest, relentless and consuming. She wanted to scream, to let it out, to break something—to destroy everything that had led her to this moment.

But there was no time for that. She couldn't afford to let herself be swallowed by the grief and the anger. Not now. Not when she had come this far.

The wind outside howled, its mournful cry slipping through the cracks in the walls, an eerie sound that seemed to echo the hollow emptiness inside her. Ivy's gaze fell to the ground, where the remnants of an old tapestry lay in ruins. What had once been vibrant, full of life, was now nothing more than a pile of threadbare fabric, burnt edges curling into the air like the ghost of a forgotten dream.

She had to face this. She had to move forward, no matter how much the truth stung, no matter how much the weight of it pressed down on her chest.

A sudden, sharp noise broke the silence. Ivy froze, her pulse leaping in her throat. Someone was here. She could feel it— a presence moving just beyond the shadows, a pair of eyes watching her every move. The hairs on the back of her neck stood on end as her mind raced, her heart pounding harder with each passing second.

"Who's there?" she demanded, her voice cracking with the tension in her throat.

The figure that stepped out from the darkness seemed almost to emerge from the walls themselves, his silhouette tall and foreboding. Ivy's breath hitched in her chest as she took a step back, her eyes narrowing.

It was him.

Her betrayer.

"You shouldn't have come," he said, his voice low, almost a whisper, but it carried in the stillness of the room like a thunderclap. His eyes—those eyes—dark, cold, and unreadable, locked onto hers with a chilling intensity. The mask he had worn for so long was gone, replaced by something far worse.

Ivy's pulse raced as a mix of fury and desperation clawed at her throat. "I've come to end this," she said, her voice steady despite the chaos inside her. "I've come to see you for what you truly are."

He smiled—a slow, cruel curve of his lips. "You don't understand, Ivy. You never did. You never understood the bigger picture."

A tremor ran through Ivy, but she held her ground. "I understand enough," she said, her voice thick with contempt. "You've used me. All along, you've been playing your game, and I've been nothing but your pawn. But not anymore."

His expression hardened, a flicker of something—resentment, perhaps—flashing in his eyes. "You think you can stop it?" he asked, his voice like gravel. "You think you can just end this? The game's already been set in motion. And now, Ivy, you are the one who will burn in the ashes."

A cold shiver ran down her spine as his words cut into her, each syllable a reminder of the truth she could no longer escape. This had never been about her. Not really. This was about power. Control. The manipulation of fate itself.

And now, she stood in the ashes of everything she had once hoped for, staring at the man who had destroyed it all.

24

The Lost Letter

The letter was still there, wedged deep in the crack of the wooden desk, hidden beneath a pile of discarded maps and forgotten scrolls. Ivy's hand trembled as she reached for it, the old parchment nearly disintegrating between her fingers. The ink was smudged, faded by time and neglect, but the weight of it—the sheer presence of the letter—pulled at her in a way she couldn't explain.

She had searched for hours, tearing through the ancient library, pulling open secret drawers and hidden compartments, her mind racing. The shadows in the corners of the room seemed to whisper, the very air heavy with anticipation. She had to find it. This letter, this one piece of evidence, could hold the key to everything. To the truth. To the betrayal she had just begun to uncover.

And yet, as her fingers brushed the delicate edge of the paper, she felt the sting of uncertainty. What if it was too late? What if the letter had already been read? What if the truth had already been twisted beyond recognition, buried so deeply that nothing could save her from the consequences of what she was about to learn?

Ivy's breath hitched in her throat. She unfolded the letter with shaking hands, the brittle paper threatening to tear with every movement. Her eyes scanned the words quickly, each letter sharp, jagged—seemingly written in haste, but also with a deliberate hand. Her heart pounded harder, louder, as she read the first line.

To my dearest Aline,

The name struck her like a blow. Aline? The woman she had been told was her mother's closest friend, the one she had always been told to trust, to admire. The same woman who had been at the center of every key decision in her life, whose words had shaped so much of what Ivy believed about herself, about the world around her.

The time has come to make a choice.

Ivy's fingers curled around the letter, her knuckles white. The words seemed to burn into her skin, a chill creeping up her spine. She continued to read, her eyes scanning quickly over the passage, absorbing every letter, every syllable.

I have watched you grow, Aline. I have seen your strength, your fire. You have been a faithful ally, but now you must understand the truth. The power that we seek is not one we can hold in our hands, but one we must control. The path we have chosen is one of shadows. And you, my friend, must take your place in it.

Ivy's breath caught in her throat. The letter was written to Aline from someone she didn't recognize—a name, perhaps, that had been erased, or simply never spoken aloud. But the words carried an unsettling weight. *The power that we seek.* That was the key, wasn't it? This had been about power all along. From the very beginning, Ivy had felt something stirring beneath the surface, a force that neither she nor anyone else could quite name.

It is time, Aline, to sever the ties that bind us to the past. We can no longer afford the luxury of mercy. There is no room for weakness in this world.

Ivy swallowed hard, her stomach churning. What was this? What had her mother—and Aline—been involved in? This letter felt like a dagger, and with every word, it drove deeper into the heart of the mystery Ivy had been desperately trying to unravel.

She could feel the walls of the room closing in, the very air thick with the weight of this secret. *There is no room for mercy in this world.* Those words hung in the air like a curse, a warning, a promise. What had been done to her? What had they planned?

I have already set things in motion, Aline. The one you cherish most will be the one to pay the price for the choices we are about to make. You have been warned.

The letter ended there, abruptly, the ink bleeding into a smear of black at the edge of the paper. There was no signature. No further explanation. Just a cold, heartless statement: You have been warned.

Ivy dropped the letter, her hands shaking violently now. It fluttered to the ground, its brittle edges catching the light as it landed, as if mocking her. Her heart pounded in her chest, the words reverberating in her skull. The one you cherish most.

Her mind immediately flashed to the one person who had stood by her through everything. The one person she had trusted beyond all others. Her heart clenched in her chest as the realization hit her—it was him.

He was the one they meant.

Her stomach twisted in a knot of pure, undiluted terror. The room around her seemed to spin, the shadows stretching long and menacing. Every memory she had shared with him—every moment of trust, every word of comfort—now felt like a cruel mockery, a manipulation so deep it nearly broke her.

This letter—this lost, half-forgotten piece of paper—had just shattered everything. She had walked into this place seeking answers, desperate to uncover the truth. But what she had found had left her broken, more lost than ever.

Ivy's mind raced, a thousand questions tumbling over one another. What had been set in motion? How far did this treachery go? And where did it leave her now?

The shadows in the room seemed to grow darker, pressing in around her, and for the first time, Ivy realized just how alone she truly was. In the ashes of hope, there was nothing left but the cold, unyielding grip of betrayal.

25

The Phoenix Rising

The wind howled through the narrow streets, whistling between the buildings, carrying with it the promise of rain. Ivy's steps echoed in the empty alleyway, the sound of her boots against the cobblestones the only thing breaking the silence. Her heart was heavy, her thoughts clouded with the weight of the decisions that had led her here. She had crossed every line she had once sworn she would never cross. Every step she had taken had brought her closer to a truth she hadn't been ready to face.

The letter—the lost letter—still burned in her mind, its words carving themselves into her thoughts, a constant reminder of the betrayal that had been festering in the shadows of her life. There is no room for mercy. The one you cherish most will be the one to pay the price. Ivy had read the lines over and over, but they still didn't make sense. Who was Aline truly working for? What had her mother been involved in? And what, exactly, did the letter mean by the price of her choices?

The answers felt just out of reach, slipping through her fingers every time she thought she had them. She had no choice but to press on. The road ahead was obscured by fog, but it was the only road that led to the truth, the only road that might lead her to freedom.

The entrance to the old ruins came into view, the weathered stone archway looming like a monument to the past. The place had once been a sanctuary, a place of refuge. But now, as Ivy approached, it felt more like a tomb—a mausoleum for secrets long buried. She could feel the weight of history pressing down on her, the legacy of those who had come before her hanging in the air like a curse.

Her hand instinctively reached for the dagger at her waist, the cool metal a comfort against the gnawing fear that had taken root in her chest. She didn't know what she would find inside, but she knew it would change everything. She had to be prepared.

With a deep breath, Ivy stepped through the archway and into the ruins.

Inside, the darkness was oppressive, the air thick with the scent of earth and decay. Ivy's footsteps were muffled on the dirt floor, her eyes scanning the space around her. The crumbling walls were lined with ancient carvings, symbols she didn't recognize, their meanings lost to time. But what caught her attention was the faint glow ahead—a soft, flickering light that seemed to pulse in time with her heartbeat.

She moved toward it, each step slow and measured. Her pulse quickened as she drew closer, and she saw that the light was coming from a small fire burning at the center of the room. The flames danced erratically, casting long, twisting shadows on the walls. And standing at the edge of the fire, his back to her, was the one person she had been searching for—the one who had betrayed her, the one who had set this entire tragedy into motion.

He turned at the sound of her footsteps, his eyes narrowing as he met her gaze. There was no surprise in his expression, no recognition of guilt. Just cold, detached calculation.

"I knew you would come," he said, his voice calm, even amused.

Ivy's chest tightened. "You knew?"

"Of course," he replied with a small, arrogant smile. "I've been waiting for this moment. For you to understand. To see the truth."

The flames behind him flickered again, throwing strange, flickering light across his face, making him appear both larger than life and somehow distorted. Ivy's grip on her dagger tightened. "What truth?"

He chuckled softly, a sound that sent a shiver down her spine. "That you are no longer the person you thought you were. You've been changed, Ivy. By the choices you've made. By the paths you've walked."

His words struck her like a slap. She felt the sting of them deep in her bones. Changed. She was no longer the person she had once been. The life she had known, the world she had believed in, was no longer real. Everything had been shattered, twisted, and broken.

"Why?" she asked, the word escaping her lips before she could stop it. "Why did you do this?"

His expression softened, just for a moment, before it hardened again. "I didn't do this, Ivy. You did. You made the choice. You chose to seek the truth. You chose to step into the flames." He took a step toward her, his eyes gleaming in the low light. "But like all things that are burned, you will rise from the ashes. Just like the phoenix."

Ivy stared at him, confusion and anger warring in her chest. "The phoenix?"

He nodded slowly. "Yes. The fire is your rebirth. You were never meant to be the person you were before. You've been tested, and you've survived. Now you will see the world as it truly is, and you will have the power to shape it."

The words hung in the air between them, heavy and unspoken. Ivy felt the weight of them sinking into her, filling the space around her until it was almost unbearable. Power.

She understood now. This was not just about betrayal. This was about control. About forcing her into a role she hadn't chosen, making her part of something much bigger than herself.

The flames of the fire flickered higher, casting shadows that seemed to reach for her, pulling her deeper into the web he had spun. But Ivy was no longer afraid. She had been forged in the fire. She had been burned, broken, and remade.

And now, she was ready.

With one final glance at the man who had once been her ally, she turned her back on him, stepping into the flames, the heat searing her skin as she embraced the change, ready to rise anew. The phoenix had risen.

And the world would burn with it.

26

A Dance of Ashes

The air was thick with the scent of smoke, an acrid, biting reminder of the destruction that had come before. Ivy's eyes stung, but she refused to blink. Her gaze never left him—the one who had betrayed her, the one who had dragged her into this twisted game. The flickering flames cast long, trembling shadows against the ruined walls, distorting the shapes of everything in the room.

He was standing across from her now, an unsettling calm in his posture, his face lit by the uneven glow of the fire. His expression was unreadable, his gaze sharp, almost predatory. Ivy felt the weight of the silence hanging between them, thick and suffocating. Every heartbeat echoed in her ears, a drumbeat marking the rhythm of this unholy dance they were about to share.

"You think you know everything, Ivy," he said, his voice soft yet chilling. "But you haven't even begun to understand the game you're playing."

Her pulse quickened, but she kept her stance firm. She was done with fear. Done with uncertainty. "I know enough."

He smiled, a thin, almost imperceptible curl of his lips that didn't reach his eyes. "You think this is about you, don't you? About your mother, your father... your little web of lies. But it's bigger than that. Always has been."

Ivy's breath caught in her throat. The past had always felt like a half-forgotten thing—an unfinished puzzle she could never quite piece together. Now, every word he spoke seemed to rip away the veil that had covered it. "What are you talking about?"

He took a slow step forward, and Ivy instinctively shifted her weight, her fingers tightening around the hilt of the dagger at her side. The dance had begun, and she could feel it in the air, like the pull of gravity, drawing them closer with every passing second. He moved again, and the floor creaked beneath his boots. Ivy stayed still, waiting. Watching.

"You think this ends with me, don't you?" His voice dropped lower, the words slipping through his teeth like venom. "You think that if you defeat me, you'll be free. But Ivy, you're already trapped. The moment you stepped into this world, there was no getting out. No way back. And no way forward without paying the price."

She didn't respond immediately. She couldn't. His words landed like stones in her chest, sinking deeper with every syllable. What had she been thinking? What had she been hoping for when she had followed the trail of breadcrumbs, when she had trusted the wrong people and believed the lies that had been fed to her? She had assumed that if she just kept moving forward, just kept fighting, the truth would eventually reveal itself. But now it seemed like the truth was nothing more than a dark abyss, one that threatened to swallow her whole.

"You're not the only one with power," he continued, his voice a low murmur in the tense stillness of the room. "You never have been. And the sooner you realize that, the sooner we can stop pretending."

Ivy swallowed hard, her throat dry. Every instinct told her to strike, to end this now, but something—something deep within—held her back. There was a part of her that knew that this was only the beginning.

"You think you have control," she said, her voice steady despite the rising fury inside her. "But you're wrong."

He raised an eyebrow, amused. "Am I?"

"You're nothing but a pawn. A piece in a much bigger game. And when this game ends," Ivy's words were cold, sharp, cutting through the tense air, "you'll find out just how expendable you really are."

For a moment, silence reigned, heavy and suffocating. He didn't move, didn't flinch, but Ivy could see the slight tightening of his jaw, the flicker of doubt that passed through his eyes. It was subtle, but it was there. She had struck a chord.

The fire crackled loudly in the background, the only sound in the stillness. And then, without warning, he lunged.

Ivy's heart leapt in her chest, but her training kicked in. She sidestepped just in time, feeling the brush of his sleeve as he missed her by inches. The force of his movement sent a rush of air past her, and she quickly spun, bringing her dagger into her hand. The gleam of the blade caught the light, and she steadied her breathing.

They circled each other now, like predators in the night, both of them waiting for the perfect moment to strike. His eyes locked onto hers, searching, calculating, like he could see through her. He knew her moves, her fears, the way she hesitated when the stakes grew too high.

But Ivy had learned. She had learned the price of hesitation. And this time, she wouldn't allow herself to make the same mistake.

He lunged again, this time faster, more desperate. She dodged, but his arm brushed her side, sending a jolt of pain through her ribs. She gasped, the sting sharp enough to make her vision blur for a second. But it didn't matter. She had been hurt before.

This wasn't the first time she had danced with death.

The dagger in her hand moved almost instinctively, slicing

the air as she aimed for the gap in his defense. Her strike was swift, but he blocked her with a grunt, the sound of metal meeting metal ringing through the chamber. Ivy's breath was ragged now, her movements fueled by adrenaline and sheer will. She could feel him weakening, his arrogance giving way to something more primal, something she could use to her advantage.

They clashed again, each move a symphony of chaos, a battle of wills and survival. But Ivy could see it now—the cracks in his composure, the cracks in his mask. And she would be the one to tear it apart.

With a final, sharp move, Ivy brought her blade up, aiming for his heart. The world seemed to slow as her hand guided the dagger toward its mark, the tip gleaming in the firelight.

And then, just as it seemed the blow would land, a sharp, deafening crack rang out. Ivy's world spun as the floor beneath her gave way. She was falling, the flames flickering above her as everything went black.

The game had shifted. And Ivy had just become a pawn in a far darker game than she could have ever imagined.

27

The Heart's Reckoning

The night was impossibly still, as though the world itself had paused in anticipation of the inevitable. Ivy stood in the center of the forgotten courtyard, the broken stone beneath her feet cold and unforgiving, like the truth that had been buried here for so long. The shadows around her seemed to pulse with a life of their own, stretching toward her as though reaching out to claim her, to pull her into the darkness where there was no return. The wind had died down, leaving an eerie silence that pressed in on her, suffocating her with its weight.

She could hear her own heartbeat, loud in her ears, drowning out everything else. Her hands were clenched at her sides, her breath shallow, and she could feel the tension winding tighter with every passing moment. She had come this far. There was no turning back now. But deep inside, she could feel it—the gnawing, relentless pull of uncertainty. What if she was wrong? What if everything she had fought for, everything she had sacrificed, had been for nothing?

The door creaked open behind her, and Ivy didn't need to turn around to know who it was. The air seemed to shift, the temperature dropping as footsteps echoed softly in the darkness. She didn't move, didn't even acknowledge the presence. She had known this moment was coming. And yet, standing there now, she felt a tremor of dread coil in her stomach.

"Ivy," his voice was low, hesitant, the name a mere whisper against the night air.

She turned slowly, every movement deliberate. The man who had once been her ally stood before her, his figure silhouetted against the faint light of the distant moon. His eyes were shadowed, unreadable, and for the first time in what felt like forever, Ivy saw him for what he truly was—a stranger. Not the man she had once known, not the one she had trusted, but a mere reflection of a past that could no longer be changed.

"Do you still think you can save me?" His voice cracked slightly, the words heavy with regret, but there was no trace of mercy in his gaze. No trace of the man she had loved. "After everything that's happened... Do you still believe there's a way out for us?"

Ivy swallowed hard, fighting the swell of emotions that threatened to rise up within her. She knew what he was asking. The question hung in the air, both an accusation and a plea. She had already made her decision. There was no going back, no undoing the choices they had both made.

"I didn't come here to save you," Ivy said, her voice steady, though every word felt like it was tearing her apart. "I came here to face you."

He flinched, as though her words struck deeper than any blade ever could. The silence between them stretched, thick and suffocating, until finally he stepped forward, his eyes searching hers as if trying to find something—anything—that would justify the path they had walked together.

"I never wanted this," he whispered, a touch of bitterness seeping into his voice. "I never wanted to hurt you. You have to believe me."

"You never wanted to hurt me?" Ivy's voice broke, the words sharp and accusing. "You've been lying to me since the beginning. All of it, every moment we shared, every word you said... it was all a lie."

The pain in her chest, the weight of the betrayal, finally surfaced, crashing over her like a tidal wave. She had been so blind, so naïve. How could she have trusted him? How could she have believed in the promises he made when the truth had always been right in front of her?

"I didn't have a choice," he murmured, his voice barely audible, his hands twitching at his sides. "None of us did. We were all just pawns, Ivy. The game—it's bigger than us. Bigger than anything we could control."

"Then why didn't you warn me?" she demanded, stepping closer, her fists clenched at her sides. "Why didn't you tell me the truth? You knew what was happening. You knew what I was walking into, and you just let me—"

"I couldn't!" he shouted suddenly, his voice cracking with the force of the words. "You don't understand! If I had told you, if I had tried to protect you... we would both be dead by now. You're the one who doesn't see it. This—this war, this world—it's too far gone. There's no way out. No escape."

For a moment, Ivy just stared at him, her breath catching in her throat as she struggled to process the weight of his words. The truth, the real truth, was like a weight on her chest, suffocating her, crushing the air from her lungs. There was no easy way out of this. No way to fix the damage that had been done. She could feel the old promises, the old dreams, crumbling into dust around her. And yet, in the deepest, darkest part of her heart, there was a flicker of something—a spark of defiance, of refusal to accept the end without a fight.

"I don't believe you," she said, her voice low and firm, every syllable an act of defiance. "I don't believe any of this. You've already made your choice. But I still have mine."

With that, she turned away, her eyes never leaving his as she walked toward the entrance of the courtyard. The night air seemed to grow colder as she moved, the wind picking up again, tugging at her hair, at her cloak, as though trying to pull her back into the abyss that had been set in motion long before she even understood what was at stake.

But Ivy didn't look back. She wouldn't. She couldn't.

The reckoning had come. The heart had spoken, and she would follow its call.

28

A Duel of Wills

The air had thickened, swirling with an unnatural tension. Ivy's breath was shallow, her pulse quickening with every heartbeat that reverberated through the empty courtyard. The distant howl of wind outside the stone walls was drowned out by the thunderous beating of her own heart. She stood facing him, the man who had once been her partner in all things, but now seemed like a shadow—a distorted reflection of someone she had known. The cold stone beneath her feet felt oddly steady, grounding her in the moment. She was ready, but she wasn't sure for what.

The night was darker now, the moon obscured by thick clouds that pressed down from above, making everything feel heavy, suffocating. The courtyard, once alive with echoes of joy and laughter, was now silent, save for the soft scrape of Ivy's boots against the dust. Her dagger was tucked into her belt, but she knew this confrontation would not be resolved with a blade. This was a battle of wills, and that was far more dangerous than any weapon.

He was still looking at her, his expression unreadable. But the way his jaw tightened, the way his eyes flickered with something close to regret—it told her everything she needed to know. He knew what was coming. And he knew there was no escaping it.

"I didn't want this, Ivy," he said again, his voice rough. There was a flicker of vulnerability in his eyes, a hint of the man she had once known. But it was fleeting, easily hidden beneath the mask he had worn for so long. "I never wanted to hurt you."

"You've been hurting me since the moment you decided to lie," Ivy replied, her voice steady despite the churning chaos in her gut. "Since the moment you chose this path over the truth."

His eyes narrowed, and a dark smile tugged at the corner of his lips. "You think it was a choice? You think I had the luxury of choosing? We all make sacrifices, Ivy. You, me, Aline—we all have our roles to play in this. You think you're innocent in all of this? That you're the victim?"

Ivy clenched her fists at her sides, her nails digging into her palms. "I never asked for this. But you..." Her voice cracked for a moment, but she quickly steadied herself. "You chose to drag me into your web. You chose to betray everything I believed in."

"Believe me," he said, taking a step forward. "I never wanted this for you. But you were always meant to be here. All of us were."

The words hung in the air between them, and for a moment, Ivy felt a surge of doubt, a flicker of hesitation that threatened to undo everything she had worked for. What if he was right? What if they had all been part of some grand, insidious design that none of them could escape? What if everything she had ever fought for had been a lie, and the only path forward was the one he had taken? The questions gnawed at her, trying to claw their way to the surface of her mind, but Ivy pushed them back. She would not let doubt rule her now.

Her hand slid to the dagger at her waist, and she drew it slowly, the cold metal biting against her skin. "I didn't come here to hear your excuses," she said quietly, her voice like steel. "I came here to end this."

For a moment, he didn't move, his eyes fixed on her as if he were trying to read her—trying to see if there was any trace of the woman he had once known left in her. But Ivy stood firm, her gaze unwavering. She could feel the fire burning within her, the fury and the sorrow and the desperation all churning together. But most of all, she felt something else—a deep, unshakable certainty. This was it. This was the moment.

The silence stretched between them, and then, without warning, he lunged.

The movement was fast, precise, but Ivy was faster. Her body reacted before her mind could even fully process the threat, and she twisted to the side, narrowly avoiding his outstretched hand. The edge of his cloak brushed past her face, the faintest whisper of movement as he tried to grab her.

He spun on his heel, attempting another strike, but Ivy was already there. She slashed with the dagger, the blade slicing through the air with a sharp whistle. He blocked the strike with a quick motion, his own hand reaching for her wrist, but Ivy jerked back, spinning to the side, narrowly avoiding the crushing grip.

"Is this really how you want it to end?" he hissed, his voice strained but determined. "You think you can stop me? You think you can destroy everything we've worked for?"

"I'm not destroying anything," Ivy shot back, her voice fierce. "I'm ending it. This game. This lie. And you."

The words were out before she could stop them, and she saw the flicker of disbelief in his eyes. For a brief moment, it seemed like he didn't know how to respond. He hesitated, just for a second, but it was enough.

Ivy lunged this time, her dagger aimed straight for his heart. But at the last second, he sidestepped, and the blade sank into the stone wall beside him with a sharp crack. Before she could recover, he twisted her arm, pinning it behind her back. Ivy gasped as the pressure shot through her shoulder, her body aching from the force. He held her there, the warmth of his breath against her ear, his grip unyielding.

"You think you can defeat me?" he whispered, his voice almost tender in its cruelty. "You were always just a pawn, Ivy. Just like me. Just like everyone else."

She could feel the heat of the flames growing stronger as they danced, their light flickering wildly around them. Her mind raced, her pulse roaring in her ears. She couldn't think, couldn't breathe, but somehow—somehow she knew she still had a chance. Ivy twisted with everything she had, using the weight of her body to turn, and with a sharp twist of her wrist, she broke free of his hold.

And then, in that moment of chaos, she struck.

The dagger sank deep into his side.

He gasped, his breath shuddering as he staggered back. His hand reached out to touch the wound, and when he looked at it, his fingers came away red, glistening in the firelight. His eyes met hers, wide with disbelief.

Ivy stood frozen, her breath coming in ragged gasps. The silence that followed was suffocating. In that instant, she knew that nothing would ever be the same again.

29

Fires of Desperation

The flames flickered violently in the hearth, casting long shadows across the stone walls of the chamber. Ivy stood motionless, her breath shallow and ragged as she stared at the man before her. The heat of the fire was nothing compared to the fire burning within her chest, an inferno of fury and betrayal that threatened to consume everything she had left. The room felt smaller with every passing second, the walls pressing in, closing around her. She could feel the weight of his gaze upon her, cold and unyielding.

"You don't understand," he said, his voice low but laced with a sharp edge. "None of this was ever about you. It was always bigger than that."

Ivy's heart thundered in her chest. She had heard these words before, but they no longer carried the weight of their former meaning. This wasn't some grand explanation, some hollow justification. She knew what he was trying to do—he was trying to manipulate her, to make her doubt her choices, to make her question the very foundation of everything she had fought for. But she wouldn't let him. Not now. Not after everything.

"You keep saying that," she replied, her voice tight but controlled, "but I'm not buying it anymore. I know exactly what this is about."

His lips curled into a bitter smile, his eyes glinting with something between sorrow and malice. "Do you?" he asked, stepping closer, his boots tapping softly against the cold stone. "Do you really? Do you understand that you were never supposed to know any of this? That the moment you found out the truth, you became a liability?"

The words sliced through her like a blade, and for a moment, Ivy felt the familiar pang of doubt tug at her heart. But it was fleeting. She had heard enough lies to last a lifetime. She was done listening.

"I'm not a liability," Ivy said, her voice steadier than she felt. "I'm the only one left who still has something to fight for."

He laughed softly, a hollow sound that made her skin crawl. "Fight for? You think any of this matters? You think you're the hero in this story?" His eyes darkened, and his voice dropped to a whisper, a warning that sent a chill down her spine. "You've already lost, Ivy. The fire is already burning, and there's nothing you can do to stop it now."

Ivy felt a surge of heat rise in her chest, a burning fury that matched the flames licking the edges of the room. She had heard enough of his cryptic words, enough of his twisted reasoning. She wasn't going to be his pawn any longer. She wasn't going to let him control the narrative.

"You think you can scare me?" she spat, stepping forward, her fists clenched at her sides. "You think you can make me doubt myself again? Because if you do, you've already lost."

He stopped, his expression flickering for a moment—just a moment—before he masked it again, cold and calculating. "You've always been strong, Ivy," he said quietly. "That's what makes you dangerous."

She took another step closer, her eyes never leaving his. "I'm dangerous because I'm done with the lies. And I'm done with you."

The tension between them crackled like an electric charge, the air thick with the weight of their words, their anger. She could feel her heartbeat thudding in her chest, feel the adrenaline flooding her veins as she stood there, facing the man who had once meant everything to her and now represented everything she despised.

"You still don't get it," he said, his voice barely audible over the crackling of the fire. "None of this ends well for you. You're too far in. You're too connected. They'll come for you, Ivy. They'll burn everything you love, and there won't be anyone left to save you."

Her breath caught in her throat, the familiar sting of fear creeping into her chest, but she fought it back. She had already faced the worst. She had already stared into the abyss and walked away from it. This... this was nothing. This was the final test, the moment when everything she had sacrificed would either crumble or finally come to fruition.

"And what about you?" Ivy's voice was almost too calm now, too cold. "What happens when they come for you? When you've outlived your usefulness? When you've been thrown away like everyone else you've betrayed?"

His eyes flashed, the anger in them sharp enough to cut through steel. "I told you, Ivy," he hissed. "The fire is already burning. And soon, everything you've worked for will turn to ash."

"Then let it burn." The words were a challenge, a defiance that rose up from somewhere deep within her. "Let everything burn. Because when the ashes settle, I'll be standing. And you won't."

For a heartbeat, the world seemed to hold its breath. The fire crackled, the only sound in the otherwise still room. And then, without warning, he lunged at her, his hand outstretched, his fingers reaching for her throat.

Ivy reacted on instinct, dodging to the side, her heart racing as she moved faster than she thought possible. She grabbed the nearest weapon—the iron poker from the fire—and swung it at him with all her strength. It connected with a sickening thud, the force knocking him back several paces. His expression twisted with pain, but there was no hesitation in his eyes. No retreat.

He advanced again, faster this time, a snarl of rage on his lips. Ivy's breath was coming in sharp gasps, the weight of the moment closing in on her, but she didn't hesitate. She couldn't afford to. Her arm swung, the poker catching him in the side, and she heard him grunt in pain.

But he was relentless. The fire in his eyes matched her own, burning with desperation and fury. "You don't know what you're doing," he gritted through clenched teeth.

"I know exactly what I'm doing," Ivy snapped, her pulse roaring in her ears. "I'm ending this. Once and for all."

With a final, desperate cry, he lunged again. Ivy's heart hammered in her chest as she brought the poker down with all the force she had left. The room spun as time seemed to stretch, and when the world settled again, his body crumpled to the floor, his blood staining the cold stone beneath them.

For a long moment, Ivy stood over him, her breath ragged, her body trembling. The flames continued to crackle, their warmth a cruel reminder of the price she had paid to survive this night. But as she looked down at the man who had once been her closest ally, she felt no triumph. No sense of victory.

Only the silence that came with the end of something that had never truly begun.

And the bitter, haunting knowledge that the fire was far from over.

30

The Chains of Destiny

Ivy's breath came in sharp, uneven gasps as she stood in the center of the crumbling chamber. The walls, once towering and proud, now leaned in on her like an oppressive weight, their stone surfaces etched with age and suffering. She barely noticed the dust that rose in the wake of her every movement; her focus was consumed entirely by the man standing before her, the man who had shattered her world, piece by piece. The fire in the hearth behind him flickered wildly, casting jagged shadows across his face, making him look like a wraith—a phantom of the past she could never escape.

"You can't keep running, Ivy," his voice broke the silence like a whip crack, sending a shudder down her spine. His eyes, cold and relentless, never left hers. "You can't outrun what's been set in motion. The chains are already around your wrists. There's no breaking free."

Ivy's fingers twitched at her sides, aching to reach for the hilt of her dagger, but she didn't move. She couldn't. Not yet. She had to hold on to this moment, to this fragility of time where the truth hung suspended in the air like a weapon—ready to be wielded, but waiting for the right moment.

"The chains you speak of are nothing more than lies," Ivy said, her voice barely above a whisper, but there was fire in it, a fire that matched the chaos inside her. "You think you control everything—everyone. But you're wrong."

He laughed, the sound cold and hollow, a bitter echo that seemed to reverberate off the stone walls. "You still think you have a choice, don't you? That this is something you can walk away from? No. No, Ivy. This is your destiny. Your fate was sealed the moment you chose to trust me."

Her hands curled into fists, nails digging into her palms. Every word he spoke felt like a poison, slowly seeping into her bloodstream, trying to corrupt her resolve. But she wouldn't let it. She couldn't. Not now. Not after everything.

"You've always believed that, haven't you?" she said, her voice growing steadier, more resolute. "That you were the puppet master, and I was just some marionette in your little game. But I'm done being your pawn."

For the briefest of moments, she saw something flicker in his eyes—something that resembled doubt. It was gone almost as quickly as it appeared, replaced by a look of cold determination. "You don't understand, Ivy," he said, his tone more grave now, almost pleading. "You never did. This isn't about control. This isn't about what you think you deserve. This is about survival.

About the greater good."

"The greater good?" Ivy's laugh was bitter, almost mocking. "You think I'm supposed to believe that? After everything you've done? After the lies, the manipulation, the people you've used and discarded? You don't get to talk to me about the greater good."

He took a step forward, his eyes narrowing, his lips pressing into a tight line. "You still don't understand. We don't get to choose the path we walk. The chains are there, Ivy. Always have been. And they pull us along whether we like it or not. You can fight it all you want, but it won't change anything. The world doesn't bend to our will. It bends to fate."

Ivy's chest tightened, the words rattling her as though a storm were ripping through her soul. The chains. Fate. Destiny. These were things she had never believed in, not until now. Not until the weight of the world seemed to come crashing down on her, until she realized that there was a truth buried beneath it all that she couldn't escape.

But she couldn't let him win. Not now. Not ever.

"Fate is a lie," Ivy snapped, her voice rising, cutting through the silence. "It's nothing more than a story we tell ourselves to excuse the things we can't change. I'm not going to let you dictate my future. I'm not going to let you make me believe that this is all there is."

He smirked, the dark glimmer in his eyes growing. "You don't have a choice, Ivy. You never did. You think you're free, but the chains are already around your wrists. They always have been."

The words hit her like a slap to the face, and for a moment, the room seemed to tilt around her. A cold wave of realization flooded her senses—he was right. The path she had walked had been set long before she ever realized it. She had never truly been free. She had always been a part of something larger, something that had been beyond her control.

The chains weren't physical. They were invisible, wrapped tight around her soul. They were her family's legacy, her bloodline, her decisions, the people she had trusted. Everything had been leading her here, to this moment, to this confrontation. The truth was undeniable now.

But that didn't mean she had to accept it.

"No," Ivy said, her voice low but fierce. "You think the chains bind me? You think I'm trapped? No, you're wrong. I am the one who holds the key. I can still break free."

He looked at her, his expression unreadable, and for the first time, Ivy saw the slightest flicker of uncertainty in his eyes. "You can't. It's too late for you."

She didn't flinch. Her heart was steady now, her mind clear. The chains of destiny might have bound her once, but not anymore. She had already chosen. She had already made her decision. She wasn't going to let him—or anyone—define her future.

The fire crackled behind them, the room illuminated by the harsh, flickering light. She took a step forward, her eyes locked on his, and in that moment, she knew with absolute certainty: The chains had always been there. But now, it was her turn to break them.

IV

Part Four

Ashes of Vengeance

31

The Ghost of a Lover

The wind howled through the trees, carrying with it the scent of rain, of earth and decay. Ivy stood alone in the clearing, her heart a hollow drum within her chest. The moon was hidden behind thick clouds, leaving only the faintest sliver of silver light to illuminate the world around her. The darkness felt oppressive, as though the very night itself was conspiring to swallow her whole.

She shivered, but not from the cold. There was something else here—something she couldn't quite name, but that twisted the air and made her skin crawl. It had been days since she last saw him. Days since his absence had stretched across her life like a gaping wound. The days had felt like years, each one heavier than the last, as though the very passage of time had turned against her.

And still, she could not forget him. She could not rid herself of the image of his face, the sound of his voice, the way he had once made her believe in something other than the cruel reality that surrounded them.

The sound of footsteps behind her brought her out of her thoughts, and Ivy spun around, her breath catching in her throat. The air was still again, eerily quiet, but no one was there. She could feel her pulse hammering in her neck, the hairs on the back of her neck standing on end.

"Ivy."

The whisper was barely audible, a voice from the past that she had hoped never to hear again. But it was unmistakable. The voice she had longed to forget.

Her heart lurched in her chest, and her body stiffened, the breath leaving her lungs in a rush. It couldn't be. It couldn't be him.

But when she turned, there he was.

Luca.

Standing in the shadow of the trees, his figure barely more than a silhouette in the dim light. His clothes were tattered, his face pale and gaunt, the eyes that had once been full of warmth and love now hollow, distant. He looked like a man who had walked through hell and come back a stranger, a ghost of the person he had been.

"I—I don't understand," Ivy whispered, taking a step backward. Her feet felt heavy, as though they were sinking into the ground, tethered to something far darker than the earth beneath her. "You're dead. I watched you die."

The figure in front of her smiled—a sad, twisted smile that didn't reach his eyes. "You never understood, did you, Ivy?" His voice was low, cracked, like the sound of dry leaves being crushed beneath a boot. "You never understood how much of me was always meant to die. How much of me was never really alive."

Ivy shook her head, her vision swimming. She could feel the darkness creeping in, suffocating her, and yet she couldn't look away from him. The way he stood there, so still, so unnervingly calm—it was as though time itself had forgotten to touch him. "What are you saying? How is this possible? How are you here?"

Luca stepped forward, his movements slow and deliberate, like a predator circling its prey. "I'm not here to explain, Ivy. I'm here to remind you." He reached up, running a finger along his jaw as though studying her, his eyes narrowing. "You're not free. You never were. And neither was I."

Her chest tightened, and for a moment, she couldn't breathe. "No... no, you were—" She swallowed hard, forcing the words through the lump in her throat. "You were the one person I could trust. The one person who didn't lie to me."

Luca's lips parted in something between a sigh and a laugh, and the sound sent a chill through her bones. "Trust? That was your mistake. I never wanted to lie to you, Ivy. But I wasn't strong enough to stop it. None of us were." He stepped closer, his eyes never leaving hers. "You think you've escaped the web we were caught in, but you haven't. You think you've won because you've made it this far, but you're wrong. The chains are still there, Ivy. They always will be."

Her breath came faster now, panic bubbling up in her chest. "This isn't real. You can't be real. You're dead."

A strange flicker of sadness crossed Luca's face. "Am I? Can you be so sure of that?" He reached out, his fingers brushing her cheek with an unexpected tenderness. The contact sent a jolt through her body, and she felt her pulse surge in her throat.

"I never wanted to leave you," he whispered. "I never wanted to hurt you. But you... you have to understand. You were always meant to be alone in this. Just like me."

Ivy recoiled from his touch, shaking her head desperately. "No. No, I won't believe that. I refuse to believe that."

Luca's smile faded, and his face twisted into something darker, something dangerous. "You think you have a choice? You think you're still in control? The ghosts of the past never really leave, Ivy. And neither will I."

She stepped back, her chest tightening as the weight of his words settled over her like a suffocating blanket. The truth of it hit her with a force that nearly knocked the breath from her lungs. No matter how hard she fought, no matter how far she ran, she would never be free of him—of his ghost, of his love, of the chains that had bound them both from the very beginning.

"Why are you here?" Ivy choked out, her voice trembling as she stared at the man who was no longer the man she loved. "Why come to me now? What do you want?"

Luca's form flickered, as if the very air around him was beginning to unravel. "I'm not here to hurt you, Ivy. But the past doesn't forget. And neither do I."

As the shadows closed in, Ivy stood there, paralyzed by the weight of his words, and for the first time, she wondered if there was any way out of the darkness that had followed her all these years.

32

In the Wake of Ashes

The world was silent. There were no birds calling in the trees, no rustling of leaves in the wind. The land felt still, frozen, as though even the earth itself had ceased to breathe. Ivy stood in the center of the clearing, her boots sinking into the ash beneath her feet, her heart a constant, steady drum in her chest. She could feel the weight of the silence pressing down on her, heavy and suffocating.

Around her, the remnants of the world she had known lay scattered—broken trees, charred earth, and the twisted remains of structures that had once been homes, places of refuge. But all of it was gone now. Reduced to nothing but cinders, as if the world had been burned to the ground, leaving only the ghosts of what had been.

And she was the last one left.

She wasn't sure how long she had been standing there, lost in the chaos of her own thoughts. Time had become irrelevant.

All that mattered now was the stillness that lingered, the emptiness that clung to the air. Her skin felt raw, exposed to the elements in a way that made her want to shrink back into herself, to hide from the truth that had shattered everything she once believed.

But she couldn't. Not now. Not when there was still something left to do.

Her gaze flickered to the horizon, where the remains of the castle loomed like a monument to all that had been lost. The place where everything had started, where her life had been irrevocably changed. The place where she had lost him.

Luca.

Her heart twisted at the thought of him, the memories rushing back in a flood that nearly drowned her. His face, his voice, his touch—all of it was still so vivid, so real, as if he were standing beside her. But he wasn't. He was gone. And the person standing before her now, the one who had once been her lover, was nothing more than a shadow. A hollow shell of the man she had once trusted.

He had left her with nothing but ashes. And yet, in the aftermath of everything that had happened, she knew there was still a choice to be made. The fire had burned through everything—her heart, her soul, the very foundation of her world—but it had also left something behind. Something that she couldn't ignore.

Hope.

But what was hope now? In the wake of all the destruction, what good was it? What could it possibly mean in a world that seemed intent on tearing itself apart? She didn't know. But she felt it nonetheless. A flicker of something within her, something that had been kindled deep inside her chest, refusing to be extinguished.

She couldn't explain it. She didn't even understand it herself. But it was there. And it was the only thing keeping her from falling into the abyss.

The wind picked up, swirling around her like a storm, and Ivy pulled her cloak tighter around her shoulders. She could feel the chill settling in her bones, but she didn't move. There was no escape from this place. No retreat from the truth that had been laid bare before her.

Behind her, the sounds of movement reached her ears, soft footsteps on the ash-covered ground. She turned, her breath catching in her throat as she saw him.

It was him.

Luca.

Her pulse raced, and she took an instinctive step back, her hand moving toward the dagger at her side. But it wasn't necessary. The man who stood before her was not the same one she had known. His eyes were different now—empty, hollow, the spark of life that had once burned within them extinguished long ago. He was a stranger, a ghost, the last remnants of the past she had tried so hard to bury.

"I didn't want this," his voice was hollow, a mere echo of what it once had been. "I didn't want any of this, Ivy."

Ivy's heart twisted at the sound of his voice, but she fought against the pull of those old feelings, the ones that had once made her believe in him. "You didn't want this?" she echoed, her voice tight with disbelief. "You didn't want to burn the world to the ground? You didn't want to destroy everything?"

He took a step forward, his eyes never leaving hers, and Ivy couldn't help but recoil slightly. "I never wanted to destroy anything," he said quietly. "But sometimes, Ivy, things have to burn before they can be rebuilt."

"Rebuilt?" Ivy laughed bitterly, her words choking her. "Rebuilt? There's nothing left to rebuild, Luca. There's nothing left."

He nodded slowly, as if the words themselves were a weight he had carried for far too long. "I know. And that's the problem, isn't it? We burned it all down. And now... now, we have to face the consequences."

The wind howled louder now, as if in agreement with his words, and Ivy's gaze turned to the remains of the castle in the distance, the place where it all began. She could still hear the echoes of the past there, still feel the ghost of everything that had been lost.

But as she stood there, in the wake of all that had been destroyed, something within her shifted. She didn't know what it was yet, but she could feel it—a pull toward something else, something greater than the ashes around her. Something that refused to be extinguished, no matter how hard the flames had tried to burn it away.

She didn't know where the road would lead her from here. But she knew she couldn't stay in the ashes. Not anymore.

33

The Scarlet Letter

The wind howled through the narrow passage, carrying with it the scent of damp earth and the bitter tang of iron. Ivy's footsteps echoed off the stone walls, each step growing louder in her ears as she descended deeper into the bowels of the old fortress. Her heart beat in time with the rhythm of her steps—fast, frantic, unsure. Every corner she turned, every shadow that moved in her periphery, sent her senses into overdrive. The air felt thick, charged with the weight of something—something she couldn't quite name, but knew instinctively to fear.

She had been here before, but not like this. Not with the weight of her decisions pressing down on her, not with the knowledge of what she was about to uncover. The scarlet letter—she had seen it before, a symbol of shame and dishonor, yet it had never felt more like a curse than it did now. The letter that had once been a warning had now become an inescapable truth, a truth that Ivy couldn't run from anymore. It was all coming back to her, all of it—the lies, the manipulations, the people she had trusted, the ones she had lost.

Her fingers tightened around the hilt of the dagger at her side, the cold metal a small comfort in the face of the unknown. She had come this far, past the threats and the whispers, past the ghosts of her past that had followed her like shadows. But this—this was different. This was no longer about survival. It was about choice.

The corridor ahead narrowed, and she found herself standing before a heavy wooden door, its surface scarred and worn by time. A single candle burned on the stone pedestal beside it, its flickering flame casting long shadows on the floor. The door was unmarked, but Ivy knew what lay behind it. She had known from the moment she had first set foot in this cursed place.

Her breath hitched in her throat as she reached for the handle, her fingers brushing the cool wood. The moment she touched it, she felt a pulse of heat beneath her skin, a silent warning that shivered down her spine. This wasn't a place meant for anyone who still had hope in their hearts.

With a steadying breath, Ivy pushed the door open. It creaked on its hinges, the sound deafening in the quiet of the fortress. Inside, the air was thick with the scent of stale incense and something darker, something she couldn't name. The room was dimly lit, shadows clinging to the edges of the stone walls, and the only source of light was the faint glow of a brazier in the far corner.

Her eyes immediately fell on the figure sitting at the center of the room. The figure was draped in dark robes, their face obscured by a hood. Ivy's pulse quickened. She knew who it was. She had known all along.

"You came," the voice rasped, low and familiar, as if it had always been waiting for her.

"I came to see the truth," Ivy replied, her voice steady, though her insides were a churning mass of uncertainty. "I came to see what you've been hiding."

The figure didn't move, but Ivy could feel the weight of their gaze upon her, even without seeing their eyes. The silence stretched between them, suffocating, as though the very air held its breath.

"You've always sought the truth," the voice said, almost wistful. "But truth, Ivy, is a weapon, and it is not one you are prepared to wield."

Ivy's fingers curled around the dagger's hilt once more, her knuckles white with the tension. "You don't get to tell me what I'm prepared for. Not anymore."

The figure chuckled softly, the sound sending a chill down Ivy's spine. "No, I suppose I don't. But the truth you seek... it is not the one you expect."

The hooded figure shifted then, a slow, deliberate movement, and Ivy's breath caught in her throat as the figure reached for something beside them. With a fluid motion, the figure placed a folded parchment on the stone floor, the crimson seal gleaming in the dim light.

Ivy froze. The letter. The scarlet letter.

The figure's hand lingered over it for a moment before they spoke again. "You have been carrying the weight of a lie for far too long, Ivy. It is time you see it for what it truly is."

Ivy swallowed hard. She had known this moment was coming, but the reality of it was something else entirely. The weight of the parchment in front of her felt like a burden she wasn't sure she could carry. She wanted to look away, to turn and run, but she couldn't. She had to know.

With trembling fingers, Ivy reached for the letter, breaking the seal with a sharp tear. As the parchment unfolded in her hands, her breath caught in her throat.

The words scrawled across the page were familiar—too familiar.

"You are mine, now and forever. The bloodline cannot be erased. You are the key."

Ivy's pulse hammered in her ears, her vision swimming as the words seemed to burn into her mind. This wasn't just a message. It was a warning, a binding oath that tied her to something far greater than she had ever imagined. Her fingers shook as she held the letter, the weight of its implications suffocating her.

The figure spoke again, their voice now a low whisper. "You were always meant for this, Ivy. The chains have been forged, and no matter how far you run, they will pull you back."

Ivy's breath faltered as she dropped to her knees, the letter falling from her hands to the floor. The truth she had been chasing, the truth she thought she wanted, had arrived—and it was more than she could bear.

34

A Sacrifice of Ashes

The fire crackled in the hearth, its orange glow painting the walls with fleeting shadows, but the warmth it offered was absent. Ivy stood motionless, her eyes fixed on the dark figure before her, her breath shallow in the stillness of the chamber. The heavy scent of burnt wood and ash lingered in the air, mingling with the coppery tang of blood. Everything in the room—the stone floors, the iron-rimmed windows, the faded tapestries hanging crooked on the walls—seemed soaked with the weight of secrets.

The figure before her did not speak, their presence in the room as inevitable as the coming storm. Ivy's heart pounded in her chest, each beat a reminder of how far she had come and how much she had lost. The time for hesitation was long past, yet she could not bring herself to move. The weight of the moment was too great. It suffocated her.

"You know why you're here," the voice finally broke the silence, soft yet firm, like the rustling of dead leaves. Ivy knew that voice, had known it for far too long. It was the voice of someone who had once promised to protect her, someone who had once shared her dreams and her nightmares.

But promises had long since been broken.

"I know," Ivy replied, her voice barely audible, but steady. Her throat felt dry, her chest constricting as the words formed on her tongue. "And I know what I must do."

The figure before her stirred slightly, a shadow shifting in the dim light, but they made no move to approach. Instead, they simply waited, as if they too had come to understand that this moment was beyond their control.

Ivy's gaze never left the figure. She could see the outline of the cloak, the faint gleam of silver chains that lay tangled beneath it, but it was the eyes that held her captive. Cold. Unforgiving. Eyes that had once held love, but now only reflected the ruin they had caused.

"What's the price?" Ivy asked, her voice hardening with each word. "What do you want from me?"

The figure's head tilted slightly, an almost imperceptible gesture that sent a wave of cold through her. "What do you think you have left to offer? Your soul?" There was a bitter edge to the words, like the rustling of dry paper.

Ivy shook her head, her hand instinctively reaching for the dagger at her side, fingers brushing against the hilt. She didn't need to look at it to know it was there. It had been there for so long, a constant reminder of the choices she had made. The sacrifices she had already given.

"I don't have much left," she whispered. "But I will give you what you need."

The figure's lips curled into something that almost resembled a smile, though it lacked warmth. "Good. But it is not what you think."

A chill gripped Ivy's heart. "What do you mean?"

The figure stepped forward now, the heavy cloak dragging on the ground behind them, and for the first time, Ivy saw the full extent of their presence. The hood was thrown back, revealing a face she had once known intimately—a face she had once believed she could trust. But now, it was a mask of something darker. The eyes, though familiar, held no warmth for her. Only a cold, distant emptiness.

"You cannot undo the damage you've caused," the figure said, their voice soft but chilling. "You've burned every bridge behind you, Ivy. You've killed the last part of yourself that was human."

Ivy's pulse quickened as their words sank in. The weight of the truth was suffocating. She had never been the one to run from the fire. She had always walked toward it, willing to sacrifice everything, if only it meant she could bring an end to the chaos. But now, standing before the one person who had once been her anchor, she realized how foolish she had been.

"Then what's left?" Ivy asked, her voice ragged, almost broken. "What is left for me, if everything is gone?"

The figure's expression softened for the briefest moment—just a flicker of something human—and then it was gone, replaced by the same cold indifference that had defined them. "You can't turn back now. Not after everything that has happened. The sacrifice has already been made."

A sharp pain lanced through Ivy's chest, as if a part of her soul had been wrenched free, leaving only an aching void. "What sacrifice?" she demanded, her voice rising, cracking with desperation.

The figure reached beneath their cloak and drew out something small, wrapped in worn leather. They held it out toward Ivy, and for a moment, she couldn't breathe. Her heart skipped a beat, a cold tremor passing through her. She knew what it was before they even unwrapped it. She had seen it in her nightmares.

The scarlet letter.

It was stained with blood—her blood.

Her hand trembled as she reached for it, taking the letter with fingers that felt numb, cold as ice. The weight of it in her palm was heavier than anything she had ever felt before. This was it. The moment of reckoning. The price for everything she had done.

"You asked what's left for you," the figure said, their voice now a whisper. "What's left is the cost of your choices. A life for a life. A soul for a soul."

Ivy's knees buckled beneath her, the ground seeming to tilt as she stared at the letter in her hand. The world seemed to fade away, leaving only the bloodstained parchment, and in that moment, she realized the truth. There was no going back from this. No escaping the sacrifice she had already made.

With trembling hands, Ivy opened the letter, her heart breaking as she read the final words etched into its surface.

For all that you have lost, this will be your last price. Your redemption is the fire that consumes you. You will burn as the phoenix, but you will never rise again.

The flames seemed to lick at the edges of her soul. It was done. There was nothing left but ash.

35

The Flames of Vengeance

The storm raged outside the walls of the fortress, lightning splitting the sky in jagged slashes of white-hot light, thunder roaring like the growl of some ancient beast. Inside, the room felt suffocatingly still, the air thick with the weight of impending disaster. Ivy stood alone, her hands trembling as they rested on the hilt of the sword she had taken from the armory. The metal was cool to the touch, but it seemed to burn her skin with a fire all its own.

She had never imagined it would come to this. Not this far. Not this way. But now that she was standing at the edge of this precipice, there was no turning back. She had already crossed the point of no return. The fire inside her, the fury that had been smoldering ever since the first betrayal, had grown into an inferno.

The heavy wooden door groaned open behind her, and Ivy stiffened. She didn't need to turn to know who it was. The footsteps—calm, deliberate, purposeful—were unmistakable.

Every part of her wanted to turn, to face him, to scream at him and demand answers, but the part of her that was calm, that was steely and hardened, refused to let go of the control she had fought so hard to keep.

"You came," the voice came, soft, almost amused, as though this moment was one they had been expecting all along. "I knew you would."

Ivy finally turned, her eyes meeting the cold, calculating gaze of the man who had once promised to protect her. Now, he was the one she would destroy.

"Luca," she said, her voice low but steady. "You should have stayed away."

Luca stepped into the room, his dark cloak swirling around his feet like smoke. His face was as cold as it had been the day she had watched him walk away from her. She could still feel the echo of that moment, the way he had abandoned her, left her to face the ruin of their love alone. She had once believed in him. She had once trusted him with her heart. But that man was gone now. In his place was only the ghost of a lover, a traitor wrapped in a lie.

"You misunderstand," Luca replied, his lips curving into that cold, inscrutable smile. "I didn't come here to run. I came here because I knew you wouldn't. You're too stubborn for that."

Ivy's grip on the sword tightened, and she took a step forward. Her body was shaking, but not with fear. No, this was something else. It was the flame of vengeance, and it was burning hotter with every breath.

"You've crossed the line," she said, her voice a whisper of rage. "I've given everything—my trust, my love. And you've destroyed it. All of it. For what? Power? Glory? What could possibly justify the things you've done?"

Luca's smile faltered, just for a moment, before it returned, colder than before. "You're wrong, Ivy. I didn't do this for power. I did it for survival. The world we live in is one of shadows, one where love is a weakness, and betrayal is the only path to strength. You didn't understand that. You never understood the game."

The words cut through her, sharp as a blade, but Ivy stood her ground. She was done with explanations. Done with the excuses.

"You think you're the only one who had to survive?" she said, her voice rising now, the fury building like a storm inside her. "You think I haven't fought every day of my life? You think I haven't bled for every inch I've gained? I may have been blind before, but not anymore. I see you now. I see what you've become."

Luca took a step toward her, his eyes never leaving hers. "You see nothing," he said, the words slipping from his lips like venom. "You see a version of me that never existed. The man you loved is dead, Ivy. And in his place is a creature who knows the truth of the world. The truth you've been too naïve to understand."

The truth. Ivy let the word roll over her like a wave. She had heard it too many times, each time it had been used to justify the lies, the cruelty. She had learned enough in the past few months to understand what that truth really was.

Luca wasn't the only one who had changed.

Ivy took another step forward, her sword now drawn fully. It caught the flicker of candlelight, reflecting a gleam that made it look like something alive, something hungry.

"Then let the truth be known," she said, her voice low and resolute. "This ends now."

Luca's eyes darkened, and for a moment, the façade of calm slipped. His fingers twitched, and Ivy saw the glint of a dagger at his side, but she was faster.

In one fluid motion, she lunged, her sword cutting through the air with a speed and precision that would have once been unthinkable. Luca blocked her with a swift motion of his own, but the impact sent a shock of pain through his arm. He staggered back, his dark eyes narrowing as he assessed her.

"You've learned well," he muttered, almost to himself, before his gaze hardened again. "But you're still too weak, Ivy."

"I'm not weak," she hissed. "And I'm not the girl who once trusted you."

With that, she attacked again, her sword striking with deadly intent. This time, Luca didn't block in time. The blade sliced through his cloak and grazed his side. He grunted in pain, but Ivy didn't stop. She couldn't. She had waited too long for this.

Luca's eyes flashed with a dangerous gleam, and with a roar of fury, he lunged toward her, his dagger aimed for her heart. But Ivy was ready. She twisted her body, ducking beneath his strike, and with a swift motion, drove her sword into his side. The room filled with the sound of his labored breath, the blood dripping from his wound, as he staggered back.

"Why?" she whispered, her voice trembling with the force of her emotions. "Why did you betray me?"

Luca's lips curled into a final, bitter smile. "Because, Ivy, you were never meant to be saved."

With that, the flames of vengeance consumed them both, as the storm raged louder outside, echoing the final battle that had been written in the ashes of their past.

36

The Shadow's Curse

The wind howled through the cracked windows, a mournful wail that seemed to echo Ivy's inner turmoil. Her breath came in shallow bursts as she paced the dimly lit room, her footsteps heavy on the stone floor. The walls, once solid and unyielding, now seemed to close in on her, their cold embrace a constant reminder that she was trapped. Trapped by her choices. Trapped by the past.

Her mind raced as the events of the past few days played out in her thoughts like a twisted dance. The fire that had consumed everything in its path, the lies that had been spun like threads of silk, and the faces of those she had once trusted—each of them now distorted and twisted by the truth. But it wasn't the truth that had broken her. It was the curse. The curse that had followed her, always lurking in the shadows, waiting for the right moment to strike.

She could feel it now, that dark presence, slipping into the corners of her mind. It was there when she closed her eyes. It was there when she tried to think of nothing. The curse had marked her, branded her soul, and now it demanded its price.

Ivy's hand instinctively went to the pendant around her neck, a small, delicate piece of silver in the shape of a bird with its wings spread wide. It had been a gift, a symbol of freedom, once. Now, it felt like an anchor, weighing her down. The cold metal pressed against her skin, a silent reminder that she was bound to something far darker than herself.

The door behind her creaked open, and she didn't need to turn to know who had entered. His presence was as unmistakable as the storm raging outside. The air grew colder as he stepped into the room, and Ivy felt the weight of his gaze upon her, sharp and unyielding.

"You've been avoiding me," Luca's voice cut through the stillness, low and dangerous. "I don't appreciate being ignored, Ivy."

She didn't respond immediately, but the muscles in her back tightened, her fingers tightening around the pendant as though it could offer her some kind of protection. The last time she had faced him, there had been fire. There had been rage. But now... now, there was only a quiet, unbearable dread.

"You've been avoiding your own fate," Ivy said quietly, her voice carrying a weight she hadn't intended. She didn't turn to face him. She couldn't. Not yet.

Luca chuckled, a sound that sent a cold shiver down her spine.

"Fate? No, Ivy. Fate is a lie. It's a story told by those who are weak enough to believe it. What you're feeling is not fate, it's fear."

Fear.

The word rattled in her chest like a rattlesnake's warning rattle. She had feared many things in her life—the dark corners of the world, the whispers of enemies hidden in plain sight, the betrayal that had sliced through her like a blade. But this? This was different. This was the shadow of something much older, something far darker than anything she had ever known.

The curse.

She could feel it pressing in, tugging at the edges of her consciousness, threatening to pull her into the depths where no light could reach. It had been with her for years, since that night in the woods, when everything had changed. Since she had made the choice that had bound her soul to something darker than death itself. And now, the price was coming due.

"Why are you here?" she whispered, her voice barely audible. Her fingers trembled as she reached for the dagger at her side, but the cold weight of it offered no comfort.

Luca took a step forward, his shadow stretching across the floor like a living thing. "You know why I'm here, Ivy. You've always known."

Her chest tightened, her heart hammering against her ribs.

The shadow. It was his doing. Everything that had happened—the fire, the bloodshed, the lies—it had all been a part of his game. A game he had played for far too long.

"I can't undo it," Ivy said, her voice breaking as the words escaped her. "The curse... it's already taken root inside me."

Luca's eyes gleamed with something like amusement, something darker than malice. "No, Ivy. You can't undo it. Not now. Not after everything that has happened. But you can accept it. You can embrace it."

She shook her head violently, her body trembling as though the weight of the curse had finally begun to press down on her fully. "I won't."

"But you will," Luca said, his voice now cold as ice. "The curse is not something you can fight. It will consume you, piece by piece, until there's nothing left but the shadow of what you once were. And when it does, you'll be mine."

The words hit Ivy like a physical blow. The realization of what he was saying, of what he had planned all along, burned through her chest like wildfire. The curse was never about power. It was never about control. It had been about this moment. This moment where she would break, where she would become nothing more than a vessel for his darkness.

"I will not become your puppet," Ivy spat, finally turning to face him, her eyes blazing with defiance. "I will fight until my last breath."

Luca's smile widened, but there was no humor in it. Only the promise of something far more sinister. "You can try, Ivy. But you will learn, like all the others, that there is no escaping the shadow's curse."

As he stepped closer, the room seemed to darken, the air thick with the power of his words. Ivy could feel the weight of the curse around her, the invisible chains tightening with each passing second. She had no choice. The battle had already begun, whether she was ready for it or not.

And this time, there would be no turning back.

37

The Edge of Night

The moon hung low in the sky, a silver crescent lost in a sea of dark clouds, barely visible through the veil of rain that fell in sheets from the heavens. The storm had not let up. The air was thick with the scent of earth and the sharp tang of ozone, as though the very world itself was holding its breath, waiting for something—something terrible and inevitable—to unfold.

Ivy stood on the precipice, her feet unsteady on the edge of the crumbling stone wall that overlooked the ravine below. The wind tugged at her cloak, the damp fabric swirling around her legs as if to pull her deeper into the void. The noise of the storm was deafening, a cacophony of wind and rain that drowned out all other sounds, but Ivy barely noticed. Her senses were consumed by the cold, by the weight of her own thoughts, by the silent, gnawing dread that had followed her for so long.

This was it. The final moment. The last chance to make a choice.

The memories of the past few days played in her mind like a relentless tide, crashing against her thoughts, dragging her under. The discovery of the truth, the betrayal, the shattered trust—each piece of the puzzle had led her here, to this place, to this hour. She had tried to run. She had tried to fight. But now, standing on the edge of this forsaken cliff, Ivy knew that all the battles, all the bloodshed, had been for nothing. Because this... this was not a fight she could win with strength or fury. This was the culmination of something older, something far darker than she had ever understood.

The shadow had been there from the beginning, always lurking, always waiting, feeding on her doubts and her fears. It had been there in the cracks of her memories, in the whispers in the dark corners of her mind, in the moments when she thought she had nothing left to lose. It had always been there.

"You can't escape it, Ivy."

The voice came from behind her, low and steady, as though its owner had known all along that this moment would come. Ivy's body tensed, her hand instinctively reaching for the dagger at her side. But she didn't turn. She couldn't. She had already known who it was. The voice, the presence, the familiarity—it all pointed to one inescapable truth.

Luca.

"Why are you doing this?" Ivy's voice was barely a whisper, carried away by the wind, but the question hung in the air between them like a fragile thread.

"Doing what?" Luca replied, his voice calm, devoid of any emotion that might reveal his true feelings. "What you're doing is far more important than anything I could do. This was always meant to happen, Ivy. You were never going to escape."

Her grip tightened on the dagger, but it was a hollow gesture, as though she knew it would be useless. She had always known this was coming, hadn't she? The storm had been brewing since the moment she had crossed paths with Luca, since the moment they had made that impossible choice. There was no undoing the damage. No undoing the path they had both chosen.

"You're wrong," she said, her voice breaking with the weight of the words. "I can still choose. I can still fight." Her heart pounded in her chest, the sound of it almost deafening in the silence that had fallen between them.

Luca's footsteps were the only thing she heard now, slow and deliberate, the sound of leather boots on wet stone. His shadow stretched over her like a dark cloak, swallowing the pale moonlight.

"You think you have a choice?" His voice was now a quiet murmur, a soft promise of something terrible. "You don't. You've always been bound to the darkness. It's in your blood, Ivy. You were born to carry this curse, to walk this path. You can fight it all you want, but it will never let you go."

The wind howled, tearing at her hair, whipping the strands into her face as Ivy struggled to keep her balance. She felt the pull of the abyss below, the darkness that seemed to beckon her, urging her to step closer to the edge. The ravine yawned wide before her, its depths swallowed by shadows that seemed to stretch on forever. But it wasn't the darkness of the ravine that gripped her. It was the darkness inside herself.

Luca's words echoed in her mind, a mantra that she couldn't shake, a truth that gnawed at her soul. No matter how far she ran, no matter how hard she fought, there would always be this shadow. It would always be there, lurking in the corners of her mind, waiting to drag her under.

"I've been running from this my entire life," she whispered, more to herself than to him. "But maybe... maybe it's time I stopped running."

Luca took another step forward, his breath cool against the back of her neck. His presence was suffocating, but Ivy didn't flinch. Not anymore.

"You're ready then," he said, almost tenderly. "Ready to embrace your fate."

She closed her eyes, the sound of the storm filling her ears, the smell of rain mingling with the scent of the earth. The darkness, the curse, the shadow—it was all a part of her now. And maybe it always had been. She had fought so long, so hard, against something that was as much a part of her as her heartbeat.

The wind whispered her name, and Ivy finally turned. Her eyes met Luca's, but this time, there was no anger, no hatred. Just resignation.

"You're right," she said softly, her voice carrying a strange calmness. "I've never had a choice. But I'll make one now."

She raised her dagger, the blade gleaming in the dim light, the reflection of the storm dancing across its edge. And for the first time in what felt like an eternity, Ivy felt no fear. Only the quiet certainty that whatever happened next, whatever darkness awaited her, she was ready to face it head-on.

38

The Red Rose

The moon hung high above the horizon, its silver light filtering through the canopy of trees, casting long shadows that seemed to stretch and reach like spectral hands. The forest was eerily silent, save for the soft rustling of leaves in the wind and the occasional snap of a twig beneath the weight of an unseen footstep. Ivy moved through the underbrush with practiced ease, her heart pounding in her chest, her every sense alert.

There was no turning back now. She had made her choice.

The red rose clutched tightly in her hand was a strange comfort, though it had once been nothing more than a symbol of everything she had lost. Its petals, dark as blood, fluttered slightly in the breeze, and the faint, heady fragrance clung to the air around her, sharp and intoxicating. She had found it just before the edge of the forest, half-hidden beneath a bed of ivy, its deep red petals a stark contrast to the dull green that surrounded it. The sight of it had made her pause, had forced her to take a breath, to remember everything she had fought for.

Everything she had loved.

Now, the rose felt like a promise—a dangerous, forbidden promise. The curse that had followed her from the very beginning was no longer just a shadow in her life. It was a part of her, inextricably tied to her soul, and as she walked through the forest toward her destination, she could feel it closing in on her, coiling around her heart like a serpent ready to strike.

Her fingers tightened around the stem of the rose as she continued to move deeper into the forest, her footsteps barely audible against the wet earth. She had to reach him. She had to confront him. There was no other choice. She had learned the truth, had seen the depths of the betrayal, and now, the only thing left to do was to face it—head-on.

The trees grew taller and thicker as she moved further into the forest, their twisted branches forming a canopy so dense that little light pierced through. The air grew colder, the humidity thick and oppressive, but Ivy barely noticed. Her thoughts were elsewhere, consumed by the knowledge of what was to come.

Finally, after what felt like hours of walking in silence, she came upon a small clearing, the ground soft and overgrown with moss. At the center of the clearing was a stone altar, ancient and weathered by time, its surface etched with strange, cryptic symbols. The air around it seemed to hum, a low vibration that resonated deep in her chest, and Ivy's pulse quickened. She had been here before. Not physically, but in her dreams, in the fragments of memories that had always felt like echoes from another life.

And there, standing in the shadows beside the altar, was Luca.

His figure was dark against the moonlight, his features barely discernible except for the flash of his pale eyes, gleaming like twin shards of ice. He didn't move as she stepped forward, didn't speak, didn't acknowledge her presence. It was as though he were waiting for her to come to him, to make the first move.

"I came," Ivy said, her voice cutting through the silence like a knife. Her hand still gripped the red rose tightly, the thorns digging into her palm. "I came for you."

Luca's lips curved into a faint, almost imperceptible smile, but there was no warmth in it. No joy. Only a coldness that made the hairs on the back of Ivy's neck stand on end.

"You shouldn't have," he said, his voice a low murmur, rich with a knowing that made Ivy's stomach twist. "But I knew you would. The question is—why? Why come now, after everything?"

Ivy held her ground, her eyes never leaving his. "Because I've seen the truth," she said, each word deliberate, heavy with the weight of everything she had learned. "I know what you are. What you've done. And I won't let you win."

Luca's expression didn't change, but his gaze darkened, as though he were seeing right through her, to something far deeper, something far more dangerous. "You still don't understand, do you? This has never been about winning. It's about survival. About power. And about choice."

His eyes flicked to the red rose in her hand, the petals still glistening with moisture, its beauty almost too perfect. "Do you know what that is, Ivy?" he asked, his voice almost teasing. "That rose has been part of this from the beginning. You're tied to it. Bound to it. And you'll never escape it."

Ivy's breath hitched. The words sliced through her like a blade, each one cutting deeper than the last. She had thought the rose was a symbol of everything she had lost, but now, in this moment, it felt like something far more sinister. A curse. A tether. A chain that had been forged long before she had even known its weight.

"You're wrong," she said, the words burning in her throat. "I'm not bound to this. Not to you. Not to any of this."

Luca stepped forward, his movements smooth and fluid, like a predator closing in on its prey. "You say that now, Ivy," he murmured, his voice dropping lower, "but the truth is, you've always been mine. From the moment you stepped into this world, you've been part of the game. You're just too blind to see it."

Before she could react, Luca's hand shot out, and Ivy barely had time to react before he seized the rose from her grasp. For a moment, she stood frozen, her heart racing in her chest, the cold air swirling around her like a vortex. He held the rose in his hand, the dark petals now stark against his pale fingers, and he looked at it with an almost reverent expression.

"You think you're in control," he said softly, his eyes never leaving the rose. "But you're not. This is your fate, Ivy. And you're already too far gone to change it."

And in that moment, with the weight of his words settling into her soul like a poison, Ivy understood. She wasn't here to save herself. She was here to confront the darkness that had been following her all along. To finally face the choice that had been set before her, whether she wanted it or not. And as Luca's smile twisted into something darker, Ivy felt the first true flicker of fear stir in her chest.

The Red Rose wasn't just a symbol. It was her curse. And now, there was no escape.

39

The Return of Fire

The sky overhead was darker than it had ever been, a blackened canvas that swallowed the stars. Not a single breath of wind stirred the air. The world seemed to hold its breath, as if everything—nature, time, and even fate itself—had paused in anticipation. Ivy stood at the edge of the ruined courtyard, her eyes locked on the distant horizon, where the faintest glimmer of orange bled through the pitch-black sky.

Fire.

It was impossible to mistake the sickly glow that flickered in the distance. She had seen it before. Felt it. The warmth on her skin, the crackling heat of destruction as it tore through everything it touched. Her stomach twisted in a knot, memories flooding her mind, but there was no time for them now. No time to remember the way it had felt when the flames had consumed her world, when the inferno had swallowed everything in its wake.

She had thought it was over. She had thought that the fire was gone, reduced to ashes, scattered to the winds. But it wasn't. It had returned, risen from the depths like some ancient, insatiable beast, ready to burn the world anew.

Her fingers trembled, but Ivy clenched her fists, forcing her body to steady itself. She had faced the flames before. She could do it again. But the burning in her chest—the ache, the fire that smoldered just beneath her ribs—told her that this time was different.

This time, it would consume her completely.

A shadow moved at the edge of her vision, and Ivy didn't need to look to know who it was. She could feel the presence as it approached, a coldness that seeped into her skin, chilling her from the inside out. Luca. Always Luca. She turned toward him, her breath catching in her throat, as though the very act of facing him summoned the heat of the fire that raged beyond.

"I knew you'd come," Luca said, his voice soft but laden with something darker. His silhouette was a sharp contrast to the firelight in the distance, and Ivy could see his eyes gleaming, pale and predatory. "You always come. To fight. To resist. But it won't matter. Not this time."

"You've always underestimated me," Ivy said, her voice quiet but firm. She took a step forward, her heart pounding, the adrenaline already beginning to surge in her veins. "I'm not afraid of fire. Not anymore."

Luca laughed, the sound low and dark, like a serpent coiling around her, tightening its grip. "Oh, Ivy. You misunderstand. The fire is not something to fear. It is something to embrace. You've always known that, deep down. You carry it with you. It's part of you."

His words struck her like a physical blow, the truth in them settling deep within her chest. The fire. The curse. It had always been there, a part of her, lurking beneath the surface, waiting for the right moment to consume her. But now, with the flames approaching, it was no longer something she could deny. It was coming for her, and there was no running from it.

The glow in the distance grew brighter, and Ivy could hear the crackle of the flames now, the sound of destruction, of everything being burned away. The heat reached her skin, a wave of blistering warmth that made her skin prickle. She clenched her jaw, forcing herself to stand tall, to face the approaching inferno.

"You can't stop it," Luca said, his voice almost a whisper now, but there was a finality in it that made Ivy's heart race. "It's too late for that. You've already made your choice."

"I've made my choice," Ivy echoed, her hand slipping to the dagger at her side. It was an old habit, but it felt right now. The weight of the blade, the familiar grip, brought some small measure of comfort. "But it's not the one you think."

Luca stepped closer, his movements graceful, like a predator circling its prey. "Is it not?" he asked, his voice low, dangerous.

"You've already walked the path I set for you. You cannot turn back now, Ivy. Not after everything."

She drew in a deep breath, steadying herself. The fire in the distance was almost upon them now, the crackling louder, the heat unbearable. But it wasn't the flames that made her hands shake. It wasn't the inferno itself that threatened to break her resolve.

It was him.

"You've always been wrong about me," she said, her voice steadier than she felt. "I never walked your path. I've always been my own."

The words rang in the silence between them, and for a moment, there was only the sound of the fire. Then, as if on cue, Luca raised his hand, and the ground beneath their feet trembled. The air shimmered, thick with power, and Ivy felt the heat surge, pressing down on her like a weight she couldn't escape.

The flames were here.

She could hear them now, roaring, crashing against the stone walls of the courtyard, licking at the edges of her resolve. Ivy's fingers tightened around the dagger, her knuckles white. The fire had always been a force of destruction, something that took everything in its path. But now, as the heat surrounded her, Ivy felt something else stir deep within her.

The flames weren't just destruction. They were rebirth.

Her heart began to beat faster, the pulse of the fire matching her own, as if they were one. The flames called to her, beckoned her to join them. She could feel them inside her now, swirling around her like an old friend, a long-lost part of herself that had been dormant for too long. This time, she wouldn't fight it. She couldn't. It was hers, as much as it was Luca's.

Ivy closed her eyes, feeling the fire rise within her, answering the call of the flames. "This is where I end," she whispered, but her voice held no fear. "And where everything begins."

The flames surged forward, and Ivy stepped into them, her heart ablaze with the return of the fire.

40

The Betrayer's Revenge

The storm had broken, but it hadn't brought any peace. Instead, a haunting quiet had descended on the world, a heavy stillness that pressed down on Ivy's chest as she stood alone in the center of the old chapel, its crumbling stone walls standing like a monument to forgotten times. The shadows stretched long across the floor, crawling toward her as if reaching for something that could never be reclaimed. Her heart drummed in her chest, each beat an echo of the pain and rage that had been building inside her for so long.

She had always known this day would come. She had known the reckoning was inevitable, but she hadn't realized how deeply it would cut. How the betrayal would twist through her, entwining itself around her heart like a blade.

The doors to the chapel creaked open behind her, and Ivy didn't need to turn around to know who it was. The scent of rain-drenched earth and smoke—an unmistakable mixture that always lingered on his skin—drifted toward her, sending a shiver of dread down her spine.

Luca.

"You came," he said, his voice cold, yet the undercurrent of something darker lingered just beneath the surface. "I knew you would."

She didn't respond. She didn't need to. The truth between them had already been spoken, though it hadn't been said aloud. She could feel it in the air, a thick tension that twisted her insides. Betrayal. His betrayal. And hers, though she couldn't quite bring herself to admit it, to say the words out loud. They both knew, though, and it was that knowledge that made her feel as though she were choking, suffocating on the weight of their shared past.

Ivy finally turned to face him, her hands balled into fists at her sides, her breath shallow. Her chest was tight with emotion—anger, confusion, sorrow—but there was no fear. Not anymore. The fear had long since drained from her, replaced by a cold resolve that she would carry to the very end.

Luca stood just inside the threshold, his dark cloak wet from the rain, his expression unreadable. He had changed since the last time they had spoken—his features sharper, his eyes colder. But the arrogance still lingered, like an invisible shield around him, and the way he looked at her... as though he already knew the outcome. It made Ivy's blood run cold.

"You know why I'm here," Ivy said, her voice barely a whisper but thick with the fury she could no longer suppress. "You know what you've done, and what it's cost me. What it's cost us."

Luca's lips curled into something between a sneer and a smile, but his eyes remained icy, distant. "What it's cost you, Ivy? You always make everything so personal. So dramatic. This is bigger than you. Than us. You were never going to be part of the final plan. You were just a stepping stone. A means to an end."

His words hit her like a physical blow, and for a moment, Ivy's knees threatened to buckle beneath the weight of them. She had known that something was off, that Luca was hiding something from her, but hearing it so plainly—hearing him admit it—was like a blow to the gut. She had never been part of the plan. Not really. She had been a pawn, nothing more than a piece on his chessboard, moved around to suit his needs.

"You lied to me," she said, her voice breaking, though she forced it to stay steady. "Everything you told me... it was all a lie."

Luca stepped forward then, his boots echoing on the stone floor, each step slow and deliberate, calculated. When he reached her, he didn't touch her—didn't need to. The space between them crackled with the tension of everything they had lost.

"It wasn't a lie, Ivy," Luca replied, his voice lower now, more intimate. "It was simply... a necessary deception. You were never meant to know the truth. Not until the time was right. And by then, you wouldn't have mattered anymore."

Ivy's eyes flashed with a sudden, ferocious light. "And now?" she demanded. "Now that you've destroyed everything, what's left for you, Luca? What is it you think you've gained? This power you've been chasing—this game you've been playing—what will it bring you when you've burned everything down to the ground?"

Luca's gaze softened for a moment, but only just. He seemed to consider her question for a long beat before he answered, his voice quiet and cold as ice.

"It brings me freedom," he said, his words simple but laden with meaning. "Freedom from the past. From the chains that bound me. And you, Ivy... you were always a part of those chains. But I've broken free. And now, I'm the one who holds the power. I hold all the pieces."

Ivy's blood ran cold. She had heard the rumors—the whispers that had followed Luca's every move in the years since their parting. There were rumors of a secret alliance, of dealings with forces darker than she had ever imagined. But hearing him speak those words, knowing that she had been nothing more than a pawn in his ruthless game, twisted something deep inside her.

"You think this is freedom?" Ivy's voice cracked, but she pushed through the pain. "What you've done—what you've become—it's nothing but a prison. A prison of your own making. And when it falls apart, when the truth finally comes crashing down on you... don't come looking for me. I'm done."

Luca's eyes darkened, the faintest flicker of something dangerous crossing his face. "You'll come back to me, Ivy. You always do. Because in the end, you're just as much a part of this as I am. You always have been. You always will be."

Without another word, he turned and disappeared into the shadows, his figure melting into the darkness like a ghost. Ivy stood frozen, her heart pounding in her chest. The storm outside had passed, but the storm inside her had only just begun. She had been wrong. Luca's revenge was not over. It had just started. And now, with the weight of betrayal hanging heavy between them, Ivy knew there was no escaping the fire that was coming.

V

Part Five

Ember's End

41

The Last Kiss

The night had fallen, but the world felt unnaturally still, as though even the stars themselves were holding their breath. The air was thick with tension, pregnant with the kind of silence that speaks volumes. Ivy stood in the center of the abandoned garden, her heart thudding in her chest, the weight of the moment pressing down on her like a storm cloud ready to burst. She hadn't expected it to end this way—not like this, not with him, not with the world they had built together now crumbling into dust.

Her fingers twitched at her sides, where the hilt of her dagger sat, cold and heavy against her skin. She had come here with one purpose—to end it. To end the lies, the betrayals, and the pain that had spiraled out of control for so long. But now, as she looked at Luca standing before her, his eyes locked on hers with a burning intensity that threatened to unravel everything inside her, she wasn't so sure.

The moonlight cut through the night like a blade, bathing the garden in pale silver light. The once-beautiful roses, now wilted and covered in frost, seemed to shudder under the weight of the cold. Ivy couldn't remember the last time the garden had felt alive. But tonight, it felt like the perfect place for a death—one final moment before everything went to ash.

Luca's figure was a shadow against the dark backdrop, his presence consuming the space between them. He was still wearing the same dark cloak that had become synonymous with him, but tonight, it looked heavier, like it carried the weight of all their shared history, their shared secrets. There was a quiet menace in his stillness, something that made Ivy's skin crawl, but also something that made her heart ache in a way she hadn't expected.

"You came," Luca's voice broke the silence, low and smooth, like a caress, yet filled with an undercurrent of something far darker. "I knew you would."

Ivy swallowed hard, her throat dry, her mouth tasting like ashes. She had to keep herself together, had to keep her mind clear. There was no turning back.

"I came because you gave me no choice," she replied, her voice steady but betraying a faint quiver. Her fingers clenched into fists at her sides. "Because you took everything from me, Luca. You used me, lied to me, and now you want me to just walk away? To pretend none of it ever happened?"

Luca's lips curled into a slow, knowing smile, but his eyes remained cold, unreadable. "I never asked you to walk away,

Ivy. I asked you to see the truth. You were never meant to be a part of this game. You never understood the bigger picture, did you?"

The words hit her like a slap. It wasn't anger that flooded her, but a deep, hollow ache, a gnawing feeling in her chest that threatened to pull her apart. Was that all she had been to him? A pawn in his endless game? A means to an end?

"Maybe I didn't understand," Ivy said, her voice tight, her fists trembling. "But I understand now. You're not the man I thought you were. And I—" Her breath hitched as the emotions surged. "I can't keep living in this lie."

Luca took a step forward then, closing the distance between them, his presence an oppressive weight. Ivy could feel the heat of him, the pull of something old and familiar that had always been there, lurking beneath the surface. His scent, the faint trace of smoke and something darker, filled her senses. His proximity sent a shiver down her spine, and for a moment, she could almost forget why she was standing there, poised on the edge of everything.

"Ivy," he whispered, his voice like velvet, but there was a chill to it that made her heart race. "You think you can walk away from me? From us? You can't. You never could."

Her chest tightened painfully. She wanted to argue, to scream at him, but the words stuck in her throat. She could feel the heat of his gaze on her, a fire that was both an invitation and a threat. The storm inside her, the fury and the hurt, were threatening to break free, but at the same time, something inside her—a faint glimmer of the woman she had once been, the woman who had loved him—begged her to pause, to listen.

Without realizing it, she took a step forward, her breath coming faster now, her mind racing as she stared into his eyes. There, deep in the coldness, she could see it—the flicker of something that hadn't fully died. Something that had once been real, before the lies and the betrayal had consumed them both.

And before she could stop herself, she reached out. Her fingers brushed against his cheek, trembling as if she were afraid he would vanish beneath her touch. Luca didn't pull away. He stood still, his expression unreadable, his breathing steady, but Ivy could feel the storm inside him, could see the conflict in the depths of his gaze.

The moment stretched out, like a slow, fragile thread between them, and before she could think, she closed the distance between them. Their lips met with an intensity that almost felt like an explosion. It was urgent, desperate, as if they were both trying to cling to something they knew was slipping away. Ivy's hands wound around the fabric of his cloak, pulling him closer, and for a heartbeat, everything else faded. The anger, the betrayal, the years of pain—they all dissolved, leaving only this one moment, this one kiss that was both an end and a beginning.

But just as quickly as it had begun, it ended. Luca pulled back, his chest rising and falling sharply, his hands gripping her arms with a force that startled her. His eyes, once soft with something like longing, were now hard, cold, and distant once more.

"You should have never come back, Ivy," he said, his voice hoarse, filled with something she couldn't place—regret, perhaps, or something darker. "But now... it's too late."

The finality in his words hit her like a wave, drowning out everything else. And for the first time, Ivy realized that some things could never be undone—not the kiss, not the betrayal, and certainly not the man standing before her.

It was over.

But in that moment, Ivy wasn't sure whether she had just lost herself, or if she had finally found the strength to let him go.

42

Into the Flames

The world had already begun to burn.

Ivy could feel it in the air, thick with the smell of smoke, the heat rising in waves as it twisted the very fabric of reality around her. The distant horizon had become a wall of fire, an inferno consuming everything in its path, devouring the world with an unrelenting hunger. It was not a natural fire; this was something darker, something that had been conjured by hands stained with too many secrets, by hearts twisted by vengeance and greed.

And yet, as the flames stretched higher, curling their fingers toward the heavens, Ivy found herself drawn to it. Drawn to the center of the storm, as if the fire had a purpose for her, something only she could fulfill. The fire that had once threatened to consume everything she held dear was now beckoning her, calling her to the heart of its fury.

She wasn't sure if she was ready to answer, but there was no turning back.

The ruins of the once-proud city stretched out before her, its buildings half-collapsed, its streets filled with the detritus of a world on the brink of collapse. There was no sign of life here, only death—the remnants of a civilization that had been torn apart by ambition and betrayal. And somewhere, buried beneath the ashes and the wreckage, was the heart of it all.

Luca.

She hadn't seen him since their last confrontation, when the truth had been revealed, when the final shattering of everything she had believed in had left her raw and exposed. But she knew he was here. She could feel his presence, a dark shadow that loomed just beyond the edges of her consciousness, always just out of reach, always watching.

But she couldn't afford to think about him. Not now. Not when the fire was this close.

Ivy pressed forward, her boots crunching against the charred ground, the heat from the flames already starting to make her skin prickle, to make her breath catch in her chest. Each step felt like a step closer to the end, and yet, as much as the fear clawed at her insides, as much as the fire seemed to pull at her soul, she couldn't stop herself. There was no escape now.

The closer she got to the heart of the blaze, the more she could feel the heat, the intense pressure that pressed down on her, as if the very air was being consumed by the flames. The walls of fire stretched around her like a cage, trapping her in a world of red and orange and black. The sound of the flames was deafening, a roar that threatened to swallow everything whole.

And yet, there was something else—something beneath the roar. A whisper. A voice calling her name, soft but insistent. It was faint at first, like the rustle of wind in a dead forest, but it grew louder, more distinct.

Ivy stopped in her tracks, her pulse racing, her breath shallow. The voice seemed to be coming from everywhere, surrounding her, pulling her closer to the heart of the flames. It wasn't Luca's voice—she would have recognized that. No, this voice was different. It was older. Wiser. It was the voice of the fire itself, the ancient power that had been awakened, the thing that had been waiting for her all along.

"Come closer, Ivy," the voice whispered, like a lover's caress, a promise and a threat all at once. "You've come so far. You've walked through shadows and blood, through lies and betrayal. And now, it is time to fulfill your destiny."

Her mind reeled. What destiny? What was it that the fire wanted from her?

But there was no time for questions. The flames were reaching higher now, lapping at her feet, curling around her ankles, as if they were testing her resolve. She could feel their warmth, the searing heat that threatened to burn her alive. And yet, it didn't hurt. Not yet. The fire wasn't meant to kill her—it was meant to transform her.

Ivy stepped forward, her heart pounding in her chest. She knew, deep down, that there was no way out of this. No way to avoid the fire that had always been inside her, the fire that had been waiting for this very moment.

The flames danced around her, teasing, beckoning her into their embrace. She didn't hesitate this time. Her hand reached out, and she stepped forward into the blaze.

For a moment, there was nothing but fire. Nothing but heat, and light, and the roar of destruction. Her vision blurred, her body consumed by the inferno as it surrounded her completely, the flames licking at her skin like a lover's kiss, hot and unforgiving.

But she didn't scream.

No, Ivy stood there, her eyes closed, her chest rising and falling with the rhythm of the flames. She felt the fire envelop her, felt it burn through her veins, through her very soul. And as it did, something inside her shifted. The fire didn't consume her—it awakened her.

A sharp pain pierced her chest, but it wasn't physical. It was something deeper, something older, as though the fire was awakening a part of her that had been buried for so long, hidden in the ashes of everything she had lost. Her breath hitched as the power surged through her, and for the first time in what felt like forever, she felt alive—truly alive, as though she were finally one with the flames.

Then, the pain faded. The fire subsided, and Ivy was left standing in the center of the blaze, her skin tingling, her heart racing, her body alive with power. The flames had tested her. But she had passed.

And now, there was nothing left but to embrace what she had become.

The fire was no longer her enemy.

It was her.

43

The Fall of Ashford

The city of Ashford was dying.

Ivy could feel it in the very bones of the earth beneath her feet. The streets, once lively with the bustling of traders and the laughter of children, now lay silent and still, the air heavy with the scent of smoke and decay. The once-proud city walls, towering and unyielding, now stood as cracked, crumbling monuments to a past that could no longer be salvaged. The fires that had begun as a distant threat were now fully upon them, licking at the edges of the city, consuming everything in their path.

Her heart pounded in her chest as she moved swiftly through the darkened streets, her every step echoing in the emptiness. The city that had once been a symbol of strength and prosperity was now reduced to ruins. The sounds of distant screams and the crackling of flames filled the air, a symphony of destruction that seemed to grow louder with each passing second.

But Ivy didn't stop. She couldn't. She had come too far, and the weight of everything that had brought her to this moment was too heavy to ignore. The truth of what had been done to Ashford, to her, and to the people she had once trusted, was now impossible to escape.

Luca had betrayed them all.

She had known it was coming, had felt it in the air long before the fires had begun to rage. But knowing something was true and seeing it unfold before her were two different things entirely. The betrayal had shattered her, broken something inside her that she wasn't sure could ever be repaired.

She could still remember the look on his face as he had turned away from her, as the last of their fragile bond had snapped. There had been no remorse in his eyes, no hesitation—only the cold, calculating determination that had always defined him. She had been nothing more than a pawn, a tool to be used and discarded. And now, the city she had once called home was paying the price for his ambition.

Ashford was burning, and with it, any hope of redemption.

Ivy's pace quickened as she neared the center of the city, where the grand citadel loomed over the surrounding buildings like a giant's shadow. The citadel was the heart of Ashford, the symbol of its power and authority. It was there that the city's leaders had once gathered, their decisions shaping the fate of the entire kingdom. But now, it was nothing more than a tomb, a monument to the arrogance and greed that had led them all to ruin.

As she approached the gates of the citadel, Ivy felt a chill run down her spine. The air here was thick with the oppressive weight of history, and the ground beneath her seemed to hum with a terrible, ancient power. The gates, once wide and welcoming, were now barred shut, a final barrier between the city's final descent into chaos and the last of its defenders.

She could see movement through the cracks in the gate, shadows shifting in the darkness. Her heart skipped a beat. Someone was inside. She didn't know who—didn't want to know—but she couldn't allow herself to hesitate. Not now. She had come too far.

With a swift motion, she drew the dagger at her side, the cold steel feeling heavy in her hand. The weapon had been with her through every step of this journey, a constant reminder of the sacrifices she had made. She had killed for it, betrayed for it, and now, she would fight with it until the very end.

Ivy pushed the gates open, her breath catching in her throat as she stepped inside the citadel's courtyard. The air was thick with smoke, and the ground was slick with the blood of those who had fallen in the streets. The sounds of battle echoed through the halls, the clash of steel on steel, the screams of the dying. But it was the silence that followed each scream that truly chilled her. Ashford's heart was beating its last.

Her eyes scanned the courtyard, searching for any sign of movement. Then, she saw him. Luca.

He stood near the base of the citadel's steps, his back to her, his dark cloak billowing in the wind, the flickering light of the fire casting an eerie glow around him. He looked almost... serene, as though he had already accepted the fall of his kingdom, as though the flames were nothing more than an inconvenience. His face was impassive, unreadable, and yet Ivy could feel the pull of his presence, the magnetic force that had always drawn her in, even when she knew better.

"Ivy," Luca's voice was soft, almost a whisper, but it cut through the chaos around them like a blade. "You've finally come."

For a moment, she couldn't move. She just stood there, staring at him, her heart torn between the memories of who he had been and the man he had become. He had been everything to her once—her partner, her lover, the man she had believed in with all her soul. And now, standing before him, she felt only a cold, empty ache.

"You've destroyed everything," she said, her voice shaking, but her words were steady. "You've burned Ashford to the ground."

He turned to face her then, his dark eyes locking onto hers with an intensity that sent a shiver down her spine. "Ashford was already dead before the fire ever touched it," he said, his voice cold, devoid of any remorse. "It was never going to survive. Not with the lies, not with the corruption. You know that as well as I do."

Tears welled up in Ivy's eyes, but she refused to let them fall. She refused to show him any weakness. "You've destroyed everything, Luca. And for what? Power? Revenge? What was all of this for?"

His lips curled into a bitter smile, and for a moment, Ivy saw the man she had once loved—the man she had once thought she knew. "I did it for us, Ivy," he said, his voice barely audible, almost too soft to hear above the raging fire. "I did it so we could be free. So we could live without the chains of this city's past. But you... you were never meant to understand."

And in that moment, Ivy realized the truth. There would be no reconciliation. No saving him. Ashford's fall was his choice, his sacrifice, and no matter how much it hurt, she would have to let him go. Let him burn.

With one last look at the crumbling city behind her, Ivy turned her back on him. There would be no final confrontation. No words left to say. Just the fire. The flames. And the ashes.

44

A Heart's Rebirth

The air was thick with smoke, and the flickering embers of a dying city clung to Ivy's skin like a reminder of everything that had been lost. Ashford's streets, once filled with life and laughter, were now a graveyard of memories. The fires had consumed the city, leaving only ruins and dust in their wake, the final act in a tragic play that had been written long before she had ever stepped onto its stage.

But even amidst the destruction, something within Ivy stirred. A flicker of light in the darkness, a spark that refused to be extinguished. The fire that had burned Ashford down had also burned away the remnants of the past—of the lies, the betrayals, the shattered promises that had shackled her for so long. And now, as she stood in the heart of the wreckage, Ivy felt something new awakening inside her.

It was as if the flames had stripped away everything false, leaving behind only the core of who she was meant to be. The woman who had walked this path of destruction, who had fought tooth and nail to survive, was no longer the same person. She had been forged in the fire, tempered by the losses and the sacrifices that had defined her journey.

And now, she was ready for the next step.

Her boots crunched on the ash-covered ground as she made her way through the charred remains of the citadel's courtyard. The grand palace that had once stood at the center of Ashford, a symbol of power and prestige, now lay in ruin, its walls crumbled and its towers reduced to smoldering skeletons. The citadel, like everything else, was broken—but Ivy could feel the pulse of something beneath it all, something still alive, something that had yet to die.

Luca was here, she knew that. He had to be. The betrayal that had set this fire in motion had begun with him, and it was fitting that it would end here, in the ashes of the city he had once claimed as his own. But Ivy no longer felt the burning hatred that had consumed her in the early days of their conflict. Instead, she felt something far more terrifying—emptiness. The fury that had driven her to seek vengeance, the pain that had clouded her vision, had given way to a quiet, unsettling peace.

And it was in this peace that she found the clarity she had been searching for all along.

Ivy paused before the great doors of the citadel, her hand trembling as she reached for the handle. She could hear the distant sound of movement from within, the soft scuff of boots on stone. But it wasn't the sound of soldiers or enemies—it was Luca. She could feel him, feel the weight of his presence pressing against her like an invisible force. It was a sensation she had learned to recognize long ago, the haunting echo of someone who had once held her heart, and then destroyed it.

The door groaned as she pushed it open, revealing the inner sanctum of the citadel. The grand hall was empty, save for the shadowed figure standing at the far end, silhouetted against the dying light. Luca. He didn't turn when she entered, his back still to her, his posture rigid, as if bracing for something.

"You came," he said, his voice cold and unyielding, but there was a trace of something else in it—something faint, a crack in the armor he had worn for so long.

"I had to," Ivy replied, her voice steady, but her heart raced in her chest. She stepped closer, each movement deliberate, calculated. "You've destroyed everything, Luca. Ashford, the people, everything we were."

"I never meant for any of it to end this way," he said, his voice softer now, almost regretful. But Ivy wasn't fooled. She had heard the lies before.

"And yet, here we are," Ivy said, the bitterness creeping back into her tone. "You played your game, and now look at us. Look at what you've done."

Luca turned slowly, his face illuminated by the flickering light of the fires outside. The lines of his features were sharper, the shadows beneath his eyes darker, as though the weight of the past had taken its toll on him too. For a moment, their eyes locked—two souls standing on the precipice of everything they had lost.

But it was the silence that followed that spoke louder than anything either of them could say. It was the silence of everything unspoken, of the things they had once shared and the things they had never said aloud.

"You've lost everything," Ivy whispered, the weight of the words sinking into her chest. "And so have I."

Luca didn't respond. He couldn't. The truth was too much for him to face, just as it had been too much for her for so long. But as Ivy stood there, staring at him, she realized something that had eluded her for so long. Their love had never been about him. It had never been about the lies he told, the betrayals he committed, or the darkness that had clouded their paths.

It had always been about her.

The woman she had become. The strength she had forged in the fires of her own pain. The woman who had survived and risen again, even when the world around her had fallen apart. It was this woman, not the girl she had once been, who stood before Luca now.

And with that realization, Ivy knew what she had to do. There was nothing left to fight for, nothing left to salvage. All that remained was the ashes.

She turned her back on him then, not out of anger, but out of something deeper, something more profound. She had been reborn in the flames, and now, she would walk away from the past, from everything that had brought her here. The fires would burn, the city would fall, but Ivy would rise.

45

The Unspoken Vow

Ivy stood in the heart of the citadel, the weight of Luca's presence more suffocating than the smoke that swirled in the air. The walls around them were scarred with the remnants of battle, the crumbling stone still warm from the fires that had ravaged Ashford. The silence between them stretched, a chasm wider than the city's destruction, and though they stood mere feet apart, it felt as if an entire world lay between them.

She could feel her pulse in her throat, each beat an unspoken question, a question that had haunted her since the moment she had learned the truth about him, since the moment she had realized that everything they had shared—everything she had believed—had been nothing but an illusion. She had wanted to hate him, to make him pay for what he had done, but the emptiness she felt inside her was colder than hatred, deeper than the grief she had expected. The fire of vengeance that had burned so brightly within her had flickered out, leaving only a hollow ache in its place.

Luca finally turned, his dark eyes meeting hers, and for the briefest moment, there was something in his gaze that made her falter. It wasn't regret. Not exactly. But it was something close to it—a brief flicker of the man he used to be before ambition had turned him into a monster, before he had betrayed everything she held dear.

"I never wanted this," he said, his voice low and heavy, the words carrying the weight of years of regret. His eyes were dark with something Ivy couldn't quite name. Pain, perhaps, or was it fear? Fear of her? Of himself?

Ivy shook her head, taking a step closer. "You didn't want this? You didn't want Ashford to burn? You didn't want to see it all crumble? You didn't want the blood of innocent people on your hands?"

Luca flinched, the accusation in her voice sharper than any blade. But there was no anger in Ivy's words. She had no more fire left for him, not for him, not for the city, not for anyone. The fire had been extinguished, and in its place was only silence.

"You don't understand," he whispered. "It wasn't supposed to be like this. None of it. I had to do it, Ivy. I had no choice. You think I wanted to betray you? You think I wanted to watch this city burn?"

"I think you never cared," Ivy shot back, her words coming faster now, spilling from her like the tears she had been holding back for so long. "I think you used me, just like you used everyone else. You—"

She stopped, her breath catching in her throat as the words died in her mouth. The memories surged, the good and the bad, the moments of tenderness intertwined with the ones where her trust had been shattered like glass. How could someone she had loved—someone she had believed in—become this thing before her? The man she had given her heart to had become a stranger, someone who had chosen the path of power over everything they had once shared.

And yet, despite everything, she couldn't bring herself to turn away. Despite the pain, the betrayal, the destruction, there was still something in her that couldn't forget the man he had once been.

"You're right," Luca said, his voice raw, a dark edge creeping into his tone. "I chose power over you, over everything we had. I thought I was doing the right thing... for Ashford. For us." He paused, his eyes never leaving hers, and for a moment, Ivy saw the ghost of the man she had once known—the man who had stood by her side, shared her dreams, and whispered promises into the night. The man who had vanished, leaving only this broken, hollow version in his place. "But I was wrong."

Ivy could feel the weight of his words like a shackle around her chest, but it wasn't enough. Nothing would ever be enough. Not now. Not after everything.

"You were wrong," she whispered, and there was no anger in her voice, only the exhaustion of a heart that had been torn in two. "But it doesn't matter anymore."

Luca's eyes flashed with something—something that looked almost like desperation. "I've lost everything, Ivy. The city, the throne, my family... But I didn't lose you. Not yet. I still have—"

"No," she interrupted, her voice firm, the finality in her words cutting through the air like a knife. "You lost me the moment you chose to burn this city, the moment you chose to destroy everything for your own gain. I'm not your salvation, Luca. I never was."

The words hung between them, heavy and suffocating, like a truth neither of them wanted to face. But Ivy knew that it was time. Time to let go of the past, time to stop pretending that there was any way to fix what had been broken. There was no redemption for him, not now. And there was no saving herself from the path she had already walked. But she could still choose to walk away.

And so she did.

Ivy turned away from him, her steps slow, deliberate, as she made her way toward the door of the citadel. The world outside was still burning, still falling apart, but Ivy felt the faintest stir of something within her—a flicker of hope. The fire had consumed Ashford, yes, but it hadn't consumed her.

And with that, Ivy made an unspoken vow to herself: she would rebuild. Not Ashford. Not what was lost. But herself. For the first time in years, she would walk away from the past, from the ashes of who she had been, and embrace the future—whatever that future might hold.

Because even in the deepest of flames, there could be a rebirth.

46

A Dark Awakening

The world felt wrong. The night air had a sharp edge to it, an unnatural chill that sank into Ivy's skin and made her bones ache. The citadel, once the proud heart of Ashford, was now a hollow shell of what it had been. The flames still smoldered in the distance, casting an eerie orange glow across the horizon, but it was the stillness—the absolute silence—that unsettled her most. It was as if the city had exhaled its last breath, and now, only the echoes remained.

She stood in the ruined courtyard, her heart pounding in her chest, her breath shallow and quick. Luca's presence lingered in the air, an invisible weight pressing against her chest, and Ivy had to force herself to take another step forward. Every instinct told her to turn away, to leave the wreckage behind, to escape before the darkness consumed her entirely. But she knew she couldn't. Not yet.

Something had changed. She could feel it in the pit of her stomach, that gnawing sense that the city's fall wasn't the end of their story. It was only the beginning.

Behind her, Luca's voice echoed in the darkness. "Ivy... please."

She closed her eyes for a moment, struggling to breathe through the knot that had formed in her throat. He was still there, still calling out to her, but his words felt distant, as if they were being spoken from across a vast chasm. There was no warmth in his voice anymore. No tenderness. Just a cold, desperate plea that only served to deepen the emptiness inside her.

When she turned to face him, she saw that he hadn't moved. His dark eyes locked on hers, but there was nothing in them now except shadows—shadows that seemed to grow deeper with each passing second. Ivy could feel it, too. The darkness that had always lurked just beneath the surface of his ambition had now fully taken root, consuming him from the inside out.

And as much as she hated to admit it, she felt a flicker of something stir inside her—a dark, unbidden sensation. It was fear, yes, but it was something more than that. It was a deep, primal recognition. Something old. Something familiar. The same hunger that had driven Luca to destroy Ashford was now tugging at her own soul.

"I thought you were gone," she said, her voice barely more than a whisper, the words trembling on her tongue.

He gave a hollow laugh, the sound dry and brittle, like the

crackling of old wood in a dying fire. "I never left, Ivy. Not really."

A shiver ran down her spine, and for the first time since this entire nightmare had begun, Ivy felt her resolve crack. She had seen what Luca was capable of. She had seen the destruction in his eyes, the way he had torn apart everything they had built, and yet, there was still a part of her—a sick, twisted part—that had believed he could be saved. That had hoped, foolishly, that the man she had once loved was still somewhere inside the monster he had become.

But now, as she looked at him, she knew the truth. There was no saving him. There was no redemption, no reconciliation. He had crossed a line that could never be uncrossed. And so had she.

The wind picked up, the ashes swirling around them like ghosts of the past. Ivy's hands clenched into fists at her sides, her nails digging into the palms of her hands. She was so close to the edge now. She could feel it, the darkness creeping into her chest, the same darkness that had consumed Luca. She could almost taste it—the bitterness of it, the seduction of it, the quiet promise that it would swallow her whole if she allowed it.

She had come to this place to destroy him. But what if, in doing so, she destroyed herself instead?

"I didn't want this," Luca said, his voice breaking slightly as he stepped closer to her. "I never wanted you to see me like this. I never wanted you to hate me."

Ivy swallowed, the words catching in her throat. "You don't get to say that to me," she whispered, her voice shaking with barely-contained fury. "You don't get to say you didn't want this when you're the one who started it. You're the one who destroyed everything, who burned this city to the ground."

"I didn't burn it all. Not yet," he replied, his gaze flickering toward the distant horizon. "The fire's still out there, Ivy. It's still waiting to consume everything, even me."

His words hit her like a blow to the chest, and she stumbled back, the weight of his admission pressing down on her like a stone. What was he saying? What was he trying to tell her?

Before she could form another thought, the ground beneath her feet trembled, a deep, resonating rumble that shook the very air. Ivy's heart skipped a beat as she looked around, her senses on high alert. The fire was coming closer, but this was something different. This was no ordinary tremor. It was as if the earth itself was reacting to the sins that had been committed upon it.

Luca's eyes flashed, his face twisted in a mixture of fear and exhilaration. "It's happening, Ivy," he breathed. "We're both part of it now. There's no way out."

And in that moment, as the ground beneath them shook and the flames drew nearer, Ivy realized the terrible truth. The darkness that had claimed Ashford had also claimed them.

There was no escaping it now. The city had fallen, but so had they.

And in the wake of that fall, they would be reborn. Not as who they once were, but as something new. Something darker. Something unstoppable.

47

The Ties That Bind

The night had fallen deeper, the silence pressing in like a suffocating shroud. Ivy stood at the center of the desolation, her body trembling with the weight of what had been done. The remnants of Ashford lay around her—burnt, shattered, unrecognizable. Once proud towers now crumbled like forgotten dreams, the city's bones scattered in the winds. The fire had ravaged the land, and yet, within her, the worst was yet to come.

She could hear him before she saw him. The scrape of his boots against the charred stone, the soft crackle of burning embers at his heels. Luca. His presence was like a storm brewing on the horizon—dark, inevitable, and terrifying.

"Ivy..." His voice was low, threaded with something that could have been regret or fear, or perhaps both. She didn't know anymore. He was a stranger now, a shadow of the man she had once known. But no matter how much the world had burned around them, no matter how much it had changed, the ties that bound them were still there, invisible but unyielding. And it terrified her.

She felt them as she turned, the weight of his gaze settling on her like a heavy cloak. It was as if the very act of meeting his eyes pulled her closer to the past, to the moments of softness that had once existed between them. There had been a time when his eyes had held warmth for her. When they had shared stolen glances and whispered promises, when the future had seemed bright. But that was before the fire, before the betrayals, before she learned the depths of his lies.

Luca stepped forward, his every movement deliberate. The shadows clung to him, the darkness woven into his very being. But beneath it all, there was a flicker—something human, something she had once held onto so tightly.

"You're still here," she said, her voice more brittle than she intended. She tried to keep the tremor from it, but it was impossible. "I thought... after everything, I thought you were gone. That you had left me here to face this alone."

He looked at her, his eyes dark and unreadable. "I never left, Ivy. Not in the way you think. I've always been here." His voice grew harder as he took another step toward her. "You know it. You've always known it."

She shook her head, stepping back. "No, I don't know anything anymore. You turned everything to ash. And now, after all of this, you still want to stand here and pretend it means something?"

The words stung, the truth behind them sharper than she could have imagined. She had spent so long trying to make sense of the man in front of her, trying to find the parts of him that were still whole, that she hadn't allowed herself to see the truth. He hadn't changed. Not really. What had changed was her. What had changed was what he had turned her into.

"I didn't want this, Ivy," Luca whispered, but there was no conviction in his voice. The words felt hollow, as empty as the city around them.

Ivy clenched her fists, her heart pounding in her chest. "You didn't want this?" she repeated, her voice rising. "You didn't want Ashford to burn? You didn't want to see everything we were slip away into nothingness? Don't tell me you didn't want this, Luca, because I know the truth." She took a step closer to him, the fire inside her rekindling, though it felt colder now, a frost that wouldn't let her go. "You did this. You made your choice, and now you have to live with it."

Luca's expression twisted, and for a moment, Ivy saw something flicker behind his eyes—guilt, perhaps, or was it a flicker of fear? She couldn't tell. But it only lasted for an instant before the mask he had worn for so long slipped back into place.

"You think I don't know that?" His voice was low, his hands balling into fists at his sides. "You think I don't wake up every damn day wondering what I've done? Wondering if it was worth it?" He closed the distance between them in a flash, his eyes burning into hers. "But the truth is, Ivy, there's no going back. And there's no undoing what I've done. The ties that bind us—they're still here, whether you want them to be or not."

The air between them crackled with tension, the kind of tension that made the world seem to stand still. Ivy could feel the weight of his words, the unspoken truth in them. There was no escaping him. Not really. No matter how far she ran, no matter how much she tried to forget, their destinies had been twisted together long ago, like threads woven into a tapestry of fire and blood.

"I hate you," Ivy said, the words breaking free of her lips before she could stop them. She hated the man he had become, hated what he had done to everything she had once believed in. She hated the power he had, the control he held over her even now.

But there was something else, something more dangerous than hate. A part of her—the part that had been buried beneath the rubble of her own heart—understood the ties that Luca spoke of. The truth was, the darkness inside him was something she had always been drawn to, something she had always been tethered to, even before she fully realized it. And now, as she faced him, she understood that the greatest betrayal had never been in his actions—it had been in the part of herself she had lost.

"Then hate me," Luca whispered, his voice rough, full of an aching vulnerability that she hadn't expected. "Hate me all you want. But don't pretend the ties are broken. Don't pretend you're not still here, standing with me, even now."

The words hung in the air between them, thick and heavy, as Ivy fought the pull of them. As much as she wanted to deny it, she could feel it—the invisible bond between them, stronger than all the fires they had lit, stronger than all the words that had been spoken. And the truth was, it was not a chain she could break. Not yet.

Not ever.

48

The Flame's End

The air was thick with smoke, heavy with the scent of burning wood and scorched earth. Ashford had once stood proud, a city of dreams and ambition, but now it was a smoldering ruin. Everywhere Ivy looked, there were remnants of a world destroyed—ruins that reflected the brokenness inside her. The fire that had torn through the city had left more than just physical damage; it had consumed everything she had known. Her trust, her heart, her very sense of self.

And now, standing in the midst of the devastation, she realized that the last ember of hope within her was flickering out, just like the flames that had ravaged Ashford.

Ivy's breath came in shallow gasps as she moved through the remains of what had once been the grand citadel. The familiar halls were unrecognizable, their once-sturdy walls now little more than charred skeletons. Each step she took echoed with finality. The echoes seemed to mock her, like the city itself was laughing at her folly, at her naïveté. She had believed in

Luca—had believed that together, they could rebuild, that love could overcome the darkness. But that was before she knew the full extent of his betrayal. Before she understood that it wasn't just Ashford that he had torn apart, but her very soul.

She stopped before what had once been the grand staircase leading up to the royal chambers. Now, the steps were nothing but blackened stone, the ornate railings reduced to twisted metal. But in the center of the courtyard, amidst the ruin, there was something that caught her eye. Something unexpected.

A single, solitary flame still burned, its orange light flickering in the night like a fragile heartbeat. Ivy's breath caught in her throat as she stepped closer, her eyes narrowing. The flame was unlike any she had ever seen before. It was smaller than the fires that had razed Ashford, but there was something unnerving about it—something too still, too quiet. As if it were waiting for something.

"Ivy."

The voice came from behind her, and she tensed, her heart leaping into her throat. She didn't have to turn around to know who it was. She could feel him, even without the sound of his footsteps. Luca.

"I knew you would come," he said, his voice low, tinged with something unreadable.

Ivy turned slowly, her eyes locking onto his. He stood there in the midst of the ruins, a figure shrouded in shadow, his face obscured by the darkness that clung to him. The firelight flickered across his features, casting half of him in light and the other half in shadow, as if the man standing before her was both a stranger and someone she had known intimately.

"You don't have to do this," Luca continued, his voice strained. "I never wanted this to happen. I never wanted to destroy everything we built. You have to believe me."

The words hung in the air between them, thick with a weight that Ivy could barely bear. But no matter how many times he said them, they didn't make sense to her anymore. The man she had loved had vanished, replaced by someone capable of destroying everything she held dear.

"I believed you once," Ivy whispered, her voice trembling. "I believed in you. And now look at this. Look at what we've become."

Luca's expression flickered, a shadow crossing his face. "I made a mistake, Ivy. But you don't have to face this alone. We can still—"

"Don't," Ivy interrupted, her voice cold, a chill settling deep inside her. "Don't tell me you want to fix this. Not after everything. Not after Ashford."

She took a step toward him, her eyes never leaving his. "You've killed this city. And you've killed us. There's no fixing it. There's no redemption for you."

The words cut through the air like a knife, and she saw the briefest flash of pain in Luca's eyes. But it was gone as quickly as it came, replaced by something harder, something darker. A finality she hadn't expected.

"I never wanted to destroy you, Ivy," Luca said, his voice tight, almost pleading. "But you have to understand—I had no choice. I made a vow. To myself. To the city. And now... there's no going back."

The words hung in the air, and Ivy felt something stir inside her, something she didn't want to acknowledge. A part of her— small, fragile—still wanted to believe in him. Still wanted to believe that the man who had once loved her, who had promised her the world, was still buried somewhere beneath the layers of lies and bloodshed.

But as she looked at him, she realized that this man—this version of Luca—was a ghost. A shadow of what he had been. And the love they once shared was gone, consumed by the flames of his ambition.

"I've already made my choice," Ivy said, her voice steady, but the words felt like a weight lifting from her chest. "And so have you."

A long silence stretched between them, broken only by the sound of the flames crackling in the distance. The heat from the fire licked at her skin, but it couldn't burn her anymore. Not like it had in the beginning.

"I have to end this," Ivy said softly, more to herself than to him. The words were like a curse, heavy and final, but she knew they were true. She couldn't keep running. She couldn't keep pretending that there was a way back.

With one last glance at Luca, Ivy turned and walked toward the flame—the last remnant of a dying world. As she reached it, the wind picked up, sending embers swirling into the air. The fire burned brighter, as if responding to her presence, and she couldn't help but think that this, too, was inevitable.

The flame would burn out. All flames did. Even the brightest ones.

But some fires, Ivy knew, could never truly be extinguished. They would always smolder beneath the surface, waiting for the right moment to ignite again.

49

The Court's Judgment

The throne room was empty, save for the three figures standing in the dim light. The once-grand hall, with its high ceilings and grand tapestries, had been reduced to a shadow of its former self. The air was thick with the smell of soot and dust, the echoes of the past lingering like ghosts among the cold stone walls. Ivy's footsteps echoed in the silence as she made her way down the aisle, her heart pounding with each step. The trial had begun, but it felt like the end—an end she couldn't quite comprehend.

Luca stood at the center of the room, his back straight, his eyes dark with resolve. He had been waiting for her, she knew. Waiting for the moment when she would be forced to make a choice, when she would have to decide whether she would stand beside him or condemn him. He wasn't looking at her now. His gaze was fixed on the judge, his posture rigid and unyielding, as if he were preparing for something inevitable.

Across from him, the judge—the figure who had once been

the voice of justice in Ashford—was silent, his face obscured by the shadow of his hood. The judge's identity had been a mystery for as long as Ivy could remember, and now, more than ever, she realized that the mystery was a curse. Because as much as she wanted to believe that this was just a trial, just a test of her loyalty, she knew it was something much darker. It was the reckoning.

"Do you understand the charges against you?" The judge's voice was low, as though the very words were too heavy to speak.

Ivy felt a coldness in her bones as she watched Luca's shoulders tense. He didn't answer immediately, his gaze unwavering. There was a quiet defiance in his stance, but also something else—something fleeting that Ivy couldn't quite place. He was afraid. And yet, it wasn't the fear of the punishment that loomed over him. It was the fear of losing her.

"I understand," he said finally, his voice even, betraying none of the emotion that churned beneath the surface.

The judge tilted his head, the movement slow and deliberate, as if weighing Luca's words. "You stand accused of the fall of Ashford. Of the destruction of its people. Of the betrayal of everything this city once stood for. And worst of all, of the betrayal of the one who trusted you above all others." The last words were spoken with a deliberate emphasis, a sharpness that cut through the air like a blade.

Ivy felt her heart falter at the mention of her name. She wanted to step forward, to speak, to explain—to somehow make sense of this twisted trial. But the words lodged in her throat, and she stood frozen, her hands clenched at her sides. The court was no longer just a place of judgment for Luca. It was a place of judgment for her too. Because somewhere, deep inside her, she knew that the true question wasn't just whether Luca deserved punishment—it was whether she did.

The silence stretched on, suffocating, until finally, the judge's voice broke through again. "Luca of Ashford, do you plead guilty to these charges?"

Luca's gaze flickered toward Ivy for the briefest of moments, his eyes softening for a fraction of a second before the mask of resolve returned. "I plead guilty," he said, the words heavy on his tongue, as if they were dragging him down into some dark abyss. "But I do not regret my actions."

Ivy's breath caught in her chest. She had known this moment was coming. Had known that he would never truly be sorry. And yet, hearing the words leave his lips felt like the final betrayal. It was as if the last thread connecting them had snapped.

"Why?" The question slipped from her mouth before she could stop it. Her voice shook, the weight of everything they had been—their love, their history, their shared dreams—crushing her. "Why did you do it, Luca? Why did you burn everything we had?"

He turned his gaze toward her, his expression unreadable. For a long moment, there was nothing but silence, as if the world itself were waiting for an answer.

"I did what I had to do," he said, his voice steady. "Ashford was broken, Ivy. We both knew it. But you—" He paused, his eyes narrowing. "You wouldn't see it. You refused to face the truth. And that... that is why I had to destroy it. To make you see."

Ivy's chest tightened. There it was—the truth, the darkness that had always been inside him. The belief that everything he did, no matter how monstrous, was justified. He had never understood the cost. He had never understood her.

The judge's voice broke through her thoughts. "The court has heard your plea. And now it will deliver its judgment."

The room grew colder, and Ivy could feel the weight of the impending decision bearing down on her. The judge turned his gaze toward her, his hooded face unreadable. "Ivy of Ashford, do you stand by this man? Do you accept his guilt, and the consequences of his actions?"

Her heart clenched. This was the moment. This was the choice that would decide everything. She had spent so long trying to make sense of it all, trying to understand why the man she had loved had turned into the very thing he had promised to destroy. But now, as she stood on the precipice of it all, there was only one thing she knew for certain: she could no longer let him drag her down into his darkness.

"No," she said, her voice trembling, but steady. "I do not."

The words hung in the air, like a death sentence, but Ivy didn't regret them. Not anymore.

50

Ashford's Reckoning

The moon hung low in the sky, casting a pale light over the ruins of Ashford. What had once been a thriving city was now little more than a broken carcass, its skeleton standing in defiance against the night. Ivy stood at the edge of the remnants of the throne room, her eyes scanning the desolate landscape. The wind stirred the ash and soot around her, but it was the silence that held her in place. There was no life here, no hope, no future. Only the echoes of the past, reverberating in the hollow spaces between the ruins.

Behind her, the trial had ended. The judgment had been passed, and yet, it felt as though nothing had been resolved. The decision to condemn Luca had been inevitable. The city had demanded it, and the people—what little was left of them— had expected nothing less. But even as the gavel had fallen, Ivy had known that the sentence wasn't just for him. It was for her too. For all that she had believed. For all the choices she had made.

Luca's fate had been sealed. The flames of Ashford had consumed everything, including his place within it. But the city's reckoning had only just begun. It was a reckoning that would come for them all, no matter how far they ran, no matter how deep they hid. Ashford was dying, and with it, the ghosts of their pasts were rising up from the ashes.

Ivy turned slowly, the weight of her own decisions pressing heavily on her shoulders. She had walked into this ruin with nothing but a heart full of hope, only to watch everything burn. The flames had taken everything she had cared for—her city, her love, her sense of self. And now, as the wind whispered through the ruins, it seemed as though the fire had not gone out at all. It had simply moved elsewhere, leaving only the faintest traces behind.

A sound broke the silence. Footsteps. Slow, deliberate. She didn't need to turn to know who it was. She could feel him, the pull of his presence like a weight on her chest.

Luca.

He had been cast out, exiled from Ashford's future, but he had returned. She should have known. He couldn't stay away. Neither could she.

"Is it done?" His voice was hoarse, as though he had been speaking for hours. Or maybe it was just the weight of the moment catching up with him.

Ivy nodded, not trusting herself to speak. What was there

to say? She had stood at his side once, had believed in his promises, in the love they had shared. But it had all been a lie—a facade built on ambition and fire. She had seen through it now, seen him for what he truly was. He was not the man she had loved. That man was long gone.

Luca stepped closer, and Ivy could feel the heat of his gaze on her, even though she refused to meet it. She had seen him burn Ashford to the ground, seen him stand as it all crumbled, and yet here he was, still alive, still standing.

"I never wanted this, Ivy," he said, his voice quieter now. "You have to believe that."

Ivy clenched her fists, the anger building up in her chest. "No. You don't get to say that anymore. You don't get to pretend that this wasn't what you wanted. You chose this, Luca. You chose the flames, and now they've taken everything. Ashford is gone, and so are we."

The words left her like daggers, sharp and final. She had come to this place of reckoning, had come to understand that there was no going back. No more pleading, no more second chances. The man who had once been her everything was now the thing she feared most.

Luca took a step closer, his expression twisted with something unreadable. "I never wanted to hurt you, Ivy. But I couldn't stop. Not then. Not when everything I ever wanted was within reach. Ashford... it was everything."

"Everything but me," she replied, her voice cold, her heart harder than it had ever been. "You used me, Luca. You used everything I believed in and destroyed it."

Luca flinched, and for a moment, Ivy saw the shadow of regret in his eyes. But it was fleeting, gone as quickly as it had appeared. He stepped back, his face hardening again, the walls he had built rising between them once more.

"Then you'll never understand," he said, his voice breaking. "You'll never understand what it took to build this, what it took to get everything we wanted. You don't know what it's like to be on the edge, to feel like everything you've ever wanted is slipping through your fingers. I did what I had to do."

"I know exactly what it feels like," Ivy said, her voice low, as the weight of the past pressed down on her. "But I would never have sacrificed everything for a lie."

There was a long silence between them, an unbearable quiet that stretched on, punctuated only by the distant sounds of the wind sweeping through the ruins. Neither of them moved. Neither of them spoke. And in that silence, Ivy realized something—something that had been gnawing at her since the flames had first begun to rise.

Ashford was gone, but its reckoning wasn't over. And neither was hers.

The ties that had bound her to Luca, to this city, were burning away, consumed by the same flames that had ravaged the streets. But even as they burned, Ivy felt something else stir within her. Something that had been buried deep, something she had ignored for far too long.

She wasn't the girl she had once been. She wasn't the naive woman who had walked into this city with hope in her heart. She was something else now—something forged in the flames of betrayal and loss. And as the last remnants of Ashford's once-proud towers collapsed into dust, Ivy knew that her reckoning had only just begun.

Luca's gaze lingered on her, but she refused to meet it. The flames had taken everything, but they had left one thing behind: herself. And that, Ivy realized, was the one thing she could still control.

Ashford was gone. And so was the man she had once loved.

But Ivy? Ivy was still standing.

And now, with the dawn of a new day, she would rise from the ashes.

51

The Shattered Heart

The night was thick with the scent of smoke and decay as Ivy stood before the remnants of Ashford's gates. The city, once a symbol of power and pride, was now a hollow shell, its spirit crushed beneath the weight of its own history. Ivy could feel the ground beneath her feet tremble, as though the city itself was mourning, shuddering with the loss of everything it had once been. The flames had not only consumed the buildings and the walls, they had consumed the very heart of Ashford.

But there was something else in the air now. A quiet, insidious presence that she couldn't shake. It clung to her, wrapped around her like a cloak, and it made her skin crawl. The feeling of being watched. The sensation that she was not alone, that there were eyes in the dark, waiting for the right moment to strike.

Her breath came in shallow bursts as she took a step forward, her heart pounding in her chest. She had made the decision. There was no turning back now. The city was lost, Ashford was lost, and so was the man she had once loved. But there was still one thing she could do. One thing she could finish.

"Ivy."

His voice was a low whisper, like the wind through the trees. It was enough to make her heart stop. She didn't turn around. She couldn't.

Luca.

"I knew you would come back." Her voice was steady, though every part of her wanted to turn and run. He had ruined everything. He had betrayed her, betrayed Ashford. He had been the fire, the one who set it all in motion, and now he was the one who would watch it burn to the ground.

Luca's shadow stretched long behind him as he stepped into the flickering light of the dying torches. His eyes were dark, his face drawn with the weight of what he had done, but there was something else in them, something harder, colder. A hunger.

"You think you can just walk away?" His voice held a strange mixture of anger and sorrow, a quiet desperation buried beneath the surface. But it was the anger that made Ivy's stomach tighten. "You think you can just leave it all behind, like nothing ever happened?"

"I don't have a choice," Ivy whispered, the words slipping from her lips like a confession. "You took everything from me. Everything I cared about. You... you ruined me."

There was a painful silence that stretched between them, long and thick with the weight of their broken past. Ivy wanted to scream at him, wanted to tear the words from his throat and make him understand the damage he had caused. But there was no point. It was too late for that. Too late for apologies, too late for explanations.

"I never wanted to destroy Ashford, Ivy," Luca said, his voice quieter now, almost pleading. "I never wanted any of this. It was never supposed to end this way. I was trying to save it—save you. Save myself."

"Save yourself?" Ivy repeated, her voice sharp. "You sacrificed everything—everyone—for your own ambition, Luca. Don't you dare tell me it was to save anyone. It was always about you. It always was."

The bitterness in her words hit him like a physical blow, and for a moment, Ivy thought she saw something like regret flash across his face. But it was fleeting. He was still Luca. Still the man who had set the world on fire, then watched it burn, leaving nothing but charred remains behind.

"I know I made mistakes," he said slowly, stepping closer. "I know I've hurt you more than I can ever undo. But, Ivy, we were meant for something greater. This... this city is nothing without us. I am nothing without you."

Ivy took a step back, shaking her head. Her hands clenched into fists, nails biting into her palms. She wanted to lash out at him, to scream at him for the lies, the betrayal. But instead, she looked at him—really looked at him. The man who had once held her heart, the man she had once thought was her salvation.

There was nothing left of him now. Nothing but the remnants of a broken soul, a heart that had been shattered long before Ashford's walls had fallen.

"Why did you do it?" she asked, her voice barely a whisper, a crack in her resolve. "Why couldn't you just love me? Why couldn't you just love Ashford?"

"I did love you," Luca said, his voice thick with pain. "But love is never enough. It's never enough when you're trying to survive. You taught me that, Ivy. You taught me that love is a weakness."

She flinched at his words, at the coldness in his voice. But there was something else there too—something that tugged at her heart. A shared past, a bond that even the flames couldn't completely burn away.

"I didn't teach you that," Ivy replied, her voice firm, though her hands trembled. "You taught yourself that. You chose to destroy everything you loved because you thought it would make you stronger."

Luca's eyes flickered with something she couldn't place. Guilt? Regret? Or maybe it was something darker. He reached out toward her, his hand trembling slightly as he tried to bridge the distance between them.

"Ivy..."

But she took another step back, her heart thundering in her chest.

"I can't, Luca. I can't go back. I can't save you."

There was a long pause. The wind howled through the remains of Ashford, a mournful sound that seemed to echo through the bones of the city itself.

"I never wanted to be saved," he said finally, his voice a shadow of the man she had once known.

The weight of those words settled over her like a death knell. Ivy's heart, already broken, shattered for the final time. There would be no redemption. No second chance. Ashford was gone, and so was the man she had once loved.

She turned away from him, her heart heavy, her mind filled with nothing but the sound of the wind and the silence that followed. The reckoning was over. And with it, so was everything.

52

Embers of Hope

The ruins of Ashford stretched before her, its charred remnants rising like a graveyard in the distance. Ivy stood at the edge of the crater where the heart of the city had once throbbed with life, and for the first time in weeks, she felt something other than the hollow ache that had consumed her. Hope—fragile, fleeting—stirred deep inside her, kindling in the ashes of everything she had lost.

The fire had burned everything. The flames had taken Ashford, had taken Luca, and had nearly taken her soul. She had watched the city burn, watched the lives of so many innocent people reduced to nothing more than smoke and cinder, and she had wondered if there was any point to going on. What was the use of surviving when the world around you had crumbled into dust?

But now, as she stood on the precipice of the city's final death, there was something different. A strange pull, a sense that the embers of Ashford were not as dead as they seemed. The fire that had torn everything apart had also forged something within her—a resilience she hadn't known she possessed.

Ivy's gaze drifted toward the ruined palace, the once-grand structure now a shell of its former glory. The windows had been shattered, the doors broken, the roof caved in under the weight of the destruction. But it was still standing. The fire had not consumed it entirely. She wasn't sure why that mattered—perhaps because it was the last remaining symbol of the city she had loved, or perhaps because it reminded her that even the most devastating forces could not completely erase what had come before.

A voice called to her from the shadows, interrupting her thoughts.

"Ivy."

She stiffened. The sound of his voice was like a jagged stone scraping against her heart. She turned slowly, the blood in her veins freezing as she saw him standing there, just beyond the edges of the firelight.

Luca.

Her breath caught in her throat, and her heart skipped a beat. He looked different now—darker, colder. His once-thick black hair was now streaked with gray, his face drawn and hollow, his eyes like twin embers glowing with something dangerous. But it was the way he stood—so sure, so unyielding—that sent a shiver through her.

"What are you doing here?" Ivy's voice came out strained, though she tried to sound stronger than she felt. She didn't want to show him how much his presence still affected her, how much the mere sight of him reopened wounds she had only just begun to heal.

"I should be asking you that," Luca replied, stepping forward. His eyes, once full of warmth and affection, now seemed distant—harder. "What are you still doing here, Ivy? This city is gone. There's nothing left for you. There's nothing left for either of us."

She swallowed the bitterness that rose in her throat. "I know what's gone. I know what you've done. But there's something else left—something I can still fight for." She looked toward the ruins of the city. "Ashford is not dead, Luca. Not yet."

He scoffed, but there was a flicker of something—recognition?—in his eyes. "You think there's still hope for this place? After everything? After what's been lost?"

"Yes," she said firmly. "There's always hope, even in the darkest of times."

Luca's gaze softened, but only for a fleeting moment. "Hope? It's a lie. It's the thing that keeps people like us tethered to a broken past, convincing us that things will get better when they never will. You and I both know that, Ivy. We've both seen too much."

Ivy's fingers clenched into fists. "I've seen what you've done.

I've seen the destruction, the lives you've destroyed. But I've also seen the people who are still standing, the ones who are still fighting. Ashford may be broken, but it's not beyond saving."

Luca took a step toward her, his voice low, filled with something she couldn't quite decipher. "And what are you going to do, Ivy? Pick up the pieces and pretend everything can be put back together? It's not that simple. You can't fix something that's already gone."

She met his gaze, her heart pounding in her chest. The pull she had felt toward him in the past—those old feelings, buried deep under layers of hurt and betrayal—were rising to the surface once more. She wanted to believe him. She wanted to believe that the man standing before her, the man she had once loved, was still somewhere deep inside. But she knew better now.

"I'm not going to fix anything, Luca. But I'm going to try," she said quietly, her voice steady. "I'm going to fight for what's left, even if it's only the smallest spark."

He stared at her for a long moment, his expression unreadable. Then, with a sigh, he turned his back on her and began to walk away. "Then you're a fool, Ivy."

"I may be a fool," she called after him, her voice rising with a newfound strength, "but I'd rather be a fool who believes in something than someone who's already given up."

Luca didn't turn around. He didn't need to. He knew she was right. And as she stood there, watching him disappear into the darkened horizon, Ivy felt the weight of everything shift. For the first time in what felt like forever, she wasn't alone. The embers of Ashford had not gone out completely. There was still fire left. And with it, there was hope.

53

A Love Reborn

The ruins of Ashford sprawled before Ivy, a silent testament to the devastation that had unfolded within its walls. Smoke still lingered in the air, a thick haze that seemed to cling to the bones of the city, as if the fire itself was unwilling to release its grip on what remained. Ivy stood at the edge of the charred marketplace, the place where she and Luca had once wandered, laughing and whispering secrets only they could understand. Now, it was a battlefield of memories, the shattered stones beneath her feet echoing with the ghosts of the past.

Her heart pounded in her chest, each beat a reminder of the weight of the decision she had made. To return here. To face him. To confront the broken pieces of their shared history. It felt like standing at the edge of a precipice, teetering on the edge of what might be the final fall.

"Ivy."

The voice came from behind her, low and almost haunting. It

was him. She didn't need to turn to know it. The sound of her name on his lips sent a shudder through her, both a pain and a longing she couldn't escape. The years of hurt, the betrayal, the loss—they all threatened to overwhelm her, but somehow, in the quiet of the ruins, she found herself turning toward him.

Luca stood in the shadow of a broken archway, his face drawn, the usual fire in his eyes dimmed. His once-pristine clothes were torn, and there was a weariness in his posture, as though the weight of everything he had done had finally caught up with him. He was not the man she had known—the man she had loved—but he was still here, still the one who had set her world on fire.

"I never thought I'd see you again," Ivy said, her voice barely above a whisper. The words felt like ash on her tongue, each one tasting like a memory of a time that was now lost. "I thought you were gone. I thought you were beyond saving."

Luca's gaze softened, but it was fleeting. He took a step toward her, the crunch of gravel under his boots the only sound breaking the silence. "I don't know if I'm beyond saving, Ivy. I don't know if I deserve to be."

The words stung, and Ivy felt a lump rise in her throat. She had spent so long hating him, blaming him for the destruction of everything she had ever loved, but now, standing here, facing him in the ruins of Ashford, she wasn't sure what to feel. Anger still simmered beneath the surface, but there was something else, something she had tried so desperately to bury.

The love they had shared—the love that had once burned so brightly—was still there. Flickering like a dying ember, but still alive. Still yearning.

"Why?" Ivy asked, her voice barely audible. "Why did you do it? Why did you destroy everything we had?"

Luca's eyes darkened, a shadow passing over his features. He took another step forward, his voice thick with emotion. "I thought I was saving it, Ivy. I thought I was saving Ashford—saving us. But I was blinded. Blinded by my own desire to fix things, to make them better. And I couldn't see the damage I was doing until it was too late."

Ivy's chest tightened. It was the answer she had always known, the one she had convinced herself wasn't true. But hearing it from him—hearing the rawness in his voice, the pain and the regret—shifted something inside her. She didn't want to forgive him. She didn't want to understand him. But she couldn't ignore the pull between them, the magnetic force that had always existed, even in the darkest of times.

"You can't just erase what you've done," Ivy whispered, her voice shaking with emotion. "You can't just come back and pretend everything is fine."

Luca's face contorted with regret, his hand reaching out as if to touch her, but he stopped short. "I know that. I know I can't undo the past. But I'm here now, Ivy. I'm here to try and make things right."

Tears welled in her eyes, but she blinked them away, angry at herself for feeling this way, for still feeling anything for him after everything he had done. But as she stood there, staring at him, she realized something—something that had been buried beneath the layers of pain and betrayal. She didn't hate him. Not anymore. She could still feel the remnants of the love they had shared, the way his presence had once made her feel like she was home, safe, whole.

"I don't know if I can trust you again," Ivy said softly, her voice trembling. "I don't know if I can ever look at you the same way."

Luca's eyes searched hers, his expression pained but resolute. "I don't expect you to. I don't deserve that. But I want to prove to you that I can change. That I can be the man you once believed I was."

The wind picked up, rustling the broken remains of Ashford, carrying with it the scent of something fresh, something new. It was as if the city, despite the devastation, was beginning to breathe again, to reclaim what had been stolen from it. And maybe, just maybe, Ivy could do the same.

"I'm not asking for your forgiveness," Luca continued, his voice steady. "I'm asking for a chance. A chance to show you that the man you loved is still in there, somewhere."

Ivy looked at him, really looked at him, for the first time in what felt like forever. The man before her was not the same as the one she had once given her heart to, but he was still Luca.

And maybe, just maybe, there was a part of her heart that still belonged to him.

"I don't know if I can love you again," Ivy said, her voice a whisper. "But I'm willing to try."

And in that moment, as the embers of Ashford burned around them, a new kind of flame sparked between them. One not of destruction, but of rebirth. Of healing. And for the first time in a long while, Ivy allowed herself to hope.

54

The Fire Within

The fire inside Ivy's chest burned hotter than the ruins around her, a relentless blaze that threatened to consume everything she had fought to rebuild. She stood in the heart of Ashford, its blackened streets stretching out before her like the scorched pages of a forgotten history. The city was still smoldering, its bones crushed beneath the weight of its own destruction. Yet somehow, amid the devastation, something in her stirred.

Her pulse quickened as she looked at Luca, who stood only a few paces away, his form silhouetted against the glow of the dying embers. He was the reason Ashford had fallen. He was the reason for all the pain. And yet, here he was, alive, breathing, his presence an unbearable reminder of everything she had lost—and everything she had once loved.

Luca's gaze was locked on her, unwavering, as if he, too, felt the weight of the moment pressing down on them both. He was waiting for something, perhaps for her to speak, to say the words that would either heal the rift between them or seal their fates forever. But Ivy's throat was tight, her breath shallow. She wanted to scream at him, to rail against the man who had broken her heart and betrayed her trust, but she found that she couldn't. There was something else inside her now, something that fought against the fury threatening to boil over.

"I didn't come here to beg for your forgiveness," Luca said, his voice rough, the words heavy with something she couldn't name. "I came here because I know what I've done. And I can't undo it. But I can't walk away either. Not from you. Not from this."

Ivy's heart lurched at the rawness in his tone. She wanted to turn away from him, to close her eyes and pretend the man who stood before her wasn't the same one who had turned his back on everything they had built together. But she couldn't. No matter how much she wanted to, she couldn't.

"Why?" she whispered, the single word laced with years of pain and confusion. "Why did you do it? Why destroy Ashford? Why destroy us?"

Luca closed his eyes for a moment, as if searching for an answer within himself. When he spoke again, his voice was quieter, more broken.

"I thought I could save it all. Ashford, the kingdom, you—us. I thought if I could just... break the chains that bound us to the past, I could build something better. Something stronger. But in trying to reshape the future, I destroyed everything. I destroyed you, Ivy. And I can't fix that."

His words hung in the air like a dense fog, and Ivy felt her anger twist into something else. Pain. Regret. Loss. Her hands clenched at her sides as the memories of their time together surged to the forefront of her mind—the laughter they had shared, the promises whispered in the quiet of the night. Those moments had been real. They had meant something. But now they were ashes, scattered in the wind.

"I didn't ask for any of this, Luca," Ivy said, her voice trembling with emotion. "I didn't ask for the pain you caused. The lies. The betrayal. And now, you stand here, telling me you can't fix it? Well, maybe that's true. Maybe you can't. But you can't just expect me to forget. You can't expect me to just... forgive you."

Luca's face twisted in anguish. "I don't want you to forgive me. Not yet. Not if you're not ready. But I need you to understand that I never meant for this to happen. I was wrong. So wrong. And if I could take it all back, I would. But I can't. All I have left is the fire inside me—the fire that's been burning ever since I realized what I've done. And all I want now is to help you, Ivy. To help you rebuild what's been broken. To help us find a way out of this darkness."

The weight of his words pressed down on Ivy, each one a dagger piercing through the layers of anger and hurt she had wrapped herself in. She closed her eyes for a moment, her breath catching in her throat. Could she really forgive him? Could she even begin to understand what he had done? It felt impossible, but as she stood there, the silence between them thick and suffocating, something inside her flickered.

She opened her eyes, meeting his gaze once more. The fire that burned in his eyes was no longer the destructive blaze that had torn through everything she had known. It was something else now. A burning need for redemption, for atonement. And it mirrored the fire within her own chest—the fire that had kept her alive, even when all she wanted to do was fall into the ashes and disappear.

"I don't know if I can ever forgive you, Luca," Ivy whispered, her voice thick with emotion. "But I can't let you burn alone. Not anymore."

Luca stepped forward, his eyes wide with disbelief. "Ivy..."

She held up a hand, silencing him. "I won't forget. I won't pretend it didn't happen. But there's a part of me—there's a part of me that still believes in what we had. In what we could still be."

Luca's breath caught in his throat as he took another step closer, his hand trembling as it reached for hers. "I've destroyed everything, Ivy. How can you still...?"

"Because you're not the only one who's burned," she interrupted, her voice steady despite the turmoil inside. "I've been in these flames too. And I know what it's like to lose everything. But if we're going to rebuild, we need to start with what's still left. And maybe, just maybe, that's us."

The fire inside her grew stronger, no longer just a symbol of destruction but of rebirth. Of hope. Of something they could still fight for. Together.

55

The Ashes of Forever

The weight of the silence stretched between them, a vast chasm that seemed impossible to cross. Ivy's breath came in shallow gasps, her heart pounding in her chest, as she tried to make sense of the chaos inside her. The city lay in ruin around them, its once grand structures now nothing more than jagged silhouettes against a sky that was slowly darkening. The fire had consumed everything, but the embers still smoldered, both in the city and in her soul.

She stood there, motionless, staring at Luca, her eyes betraying the turmoil within her. His words echoed in her mind—"I was wrong. So wrong." The words should have been a balm to her wounds, but instead, they only deepened the ache. She had spent years fighting against the memory of him, building a life in the ashes of what they once had. And now, here he was again, standing before her, offering her nothing but the truth of his regret.

Could she accept that truth? Could she ever find a way back to the man he used to be? Or had that man died along with the city, buried beneath the rubble of his mistakes?

Luca took a hesitant step forward, his gaze never leaving hers. The air between them crackled with the unspoken words they both held back, the weight of all the years, the anger, the betrayal, the loss, hanging in the balance. The flames of Ashford flickered in the distance, the city's destruction a mirror of the ruin inside her.

"Ivy…" His voice was rough, raw with emotion, and it pulled at something deep within her. But she couldn't allow herself to feel it. Not now. Not after everything that had happened.

"Stop," she said sharply, holding up a hand to halt his advance. "Don't. Don't make this harder than it already is."

Luca froze, his expression pained, but he didn't retreat. "I'm not trying to make it harder, Ivy. I'm just… trying to tell you the truth. I can't undo what I've done. But I can face it. I can face you."

She shook her head, fighting the lump in her throat. "The truth? You've been lying to me for years, Luca. You destroyed everything we had, everything I believed in. And now you think you can just show up and—what? Redeem yourself? You think you can erase the damage you've done with a few words?"

He flinched, his eyes darkening, but his voice remained steady. "I never wanted to destroy you. I never wanted to hurt you. I thought I was doing the right thing, Ivy. I thought I was saving

Ashford, saving us. But I was wrong. I was blinded by my own ambition, and I paid the price for it."

"Did you?" Ivy's words were sharp, laced with bitterness. "Did you really pay the price? You're standing here, Luca. You're alive. And I'm the one left to pick up the pieces."

The fire inside her flared, not with rage, but with a cold, bitter truth. For all his regret, for all his pain, he still had his life. He still had the chance to rebuild. But what about her? What about the pieces of her soul he had shattered? What about the years she had lost, trying to forget him, trying to move on?

"I never wanted you to pick up the pieces," Luca whispered, his voice breaking. "I never wanted you to carry this burden alone. I thought if I could fix everything, you wouldn't have to. But now... I see that I was wrong. So wrong."

Ivy's hands trembled at her sides, but she clenched them into fists, determined to hold back the tears that threatened to fall. "You can't fix it, Luca. You can't fix me. And you sure as hell can't fix what's been destroyed between us."

He took another step, closer now, until he was standing right in front of her. She could feel the heat radiating off him, the intensity of his gaze, the pull of something she couldn't name. His presence was overwhelming, suffocating, and yet, for all the fire between them, all the pain and betrayal, there was still a flicker of the man she had once loved. A part of her that wanted to believe in him again, to believe that something could rise from the ashes of their past.

"Ivy…" His hand reached out, trembling slightly, but she took a step back, instinctively pulling away from him.

"Don't," she said, her voice shaking now. "Don't touch me. Don't… don't try to fix this. It's broken, Luca. It's too broken."

He closed his eyes, his face a mask of anguish. "I know. I know it's broken. And I don't expect you to forgive me. Not now. Maybe not ever. But I will carry the weight of it for as long as I live. And if that's all I can do, then I'll do it. I will live with the ashes of what we were, and I'll never forget what I've lost."

The words hung in the air, thick with the weight of their shared history. Ivy felt a wave of exhaustion wash over her, and for a moment, she closed her eyes, allowing herself to feel the weight of it all—the years, the pain, the love that had once burned so brightly. It was gone now, reduced to nothing but memories and dust.

"I don't know if I can ever forgive you, Luca," she whispered, her voice barely audible, her heart heavy with the burden of it. "But I do know one thing."

"What's that?" he asked, his voice almost desperate.

"The ashes of forever can never be rebuilt," Ivy said, her voice cold as ice. "And neither can we."

With that, she turned away from him, her heart shattering once more, but this time, there was no fire left to burn. Only the ashes of what had once been, and the cold truth of their forever-ending.